kids say the darnest things

this book
is
MINE!

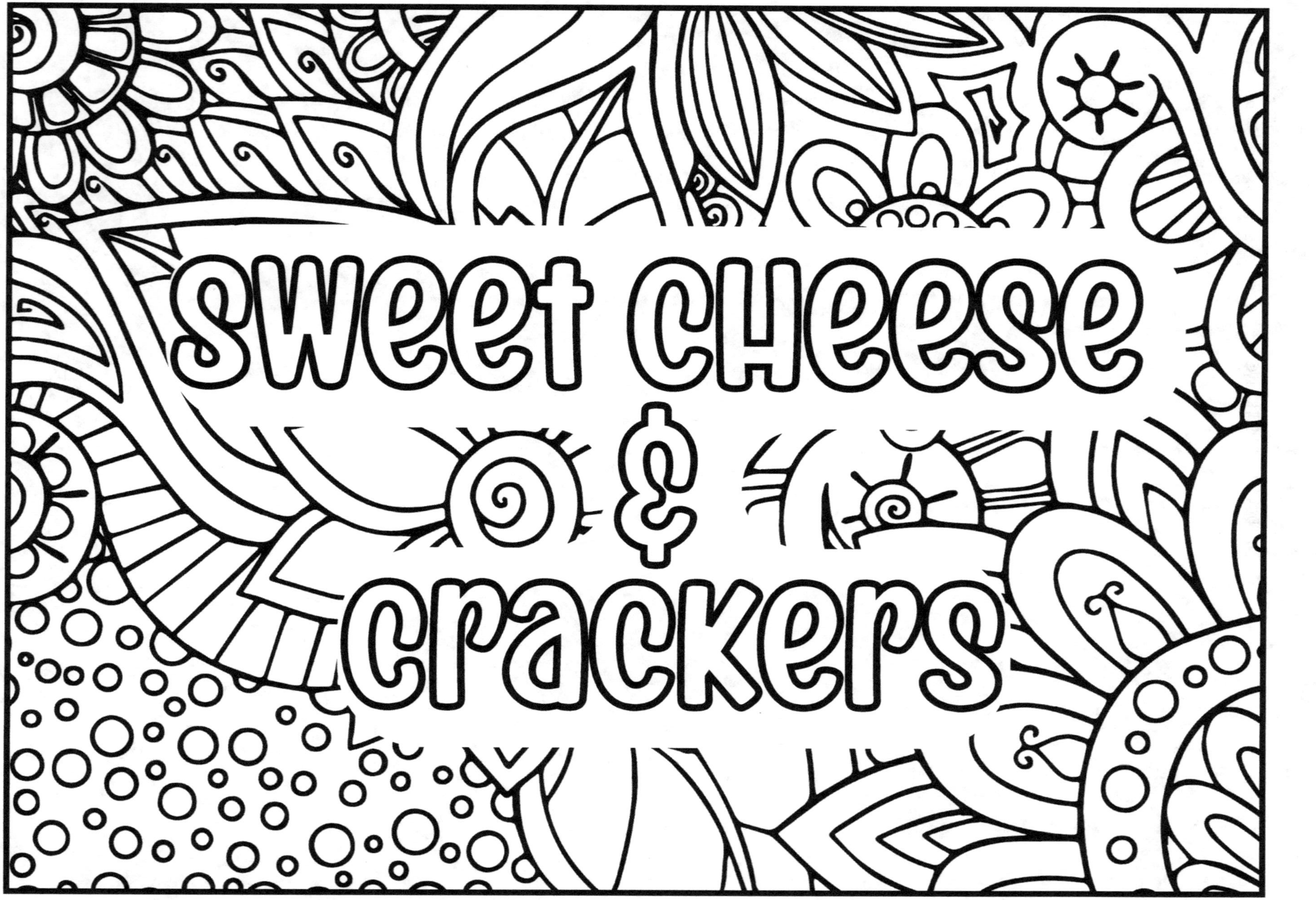
sweet cheese
&
crackers

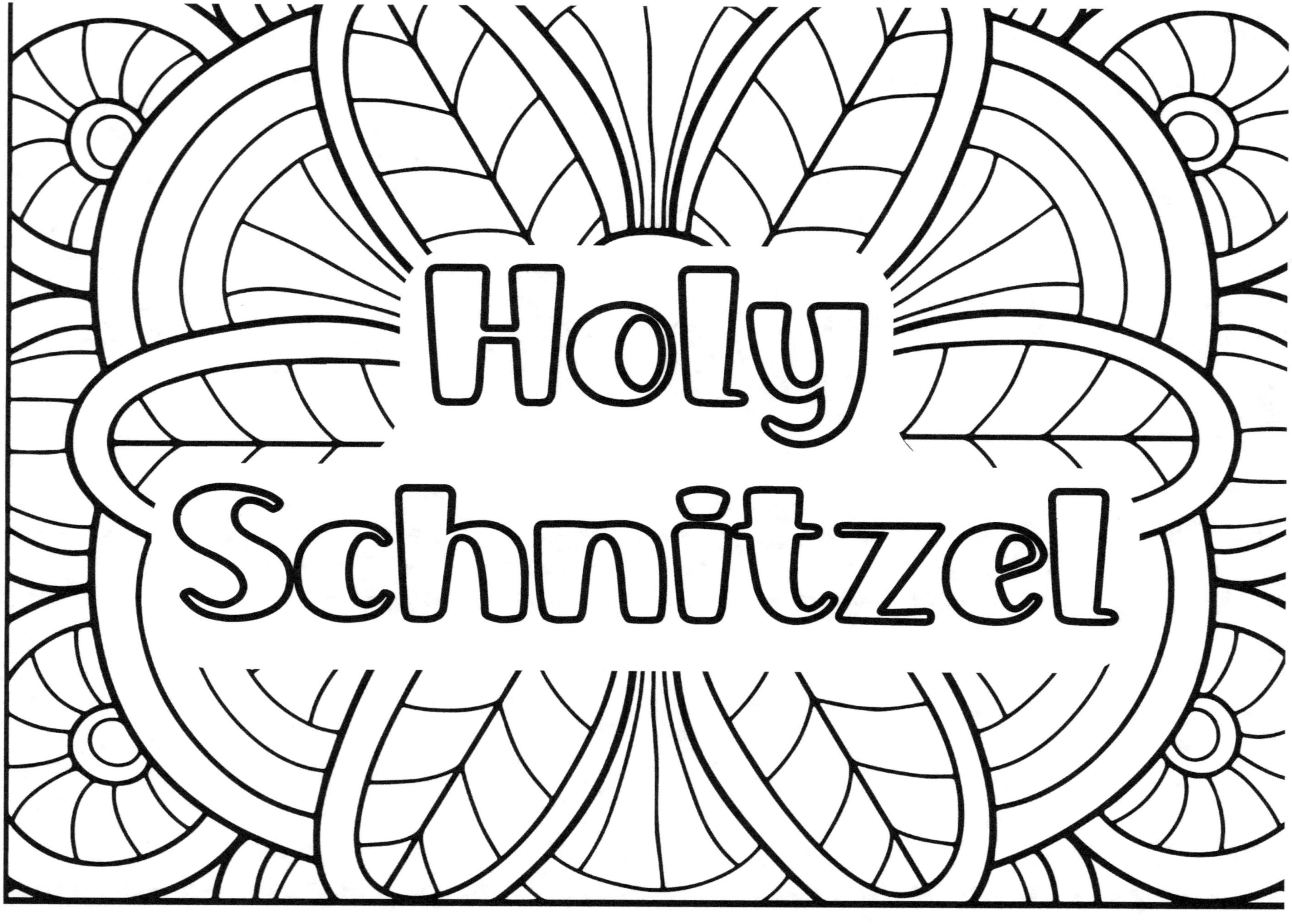
Holy
Schnitzel

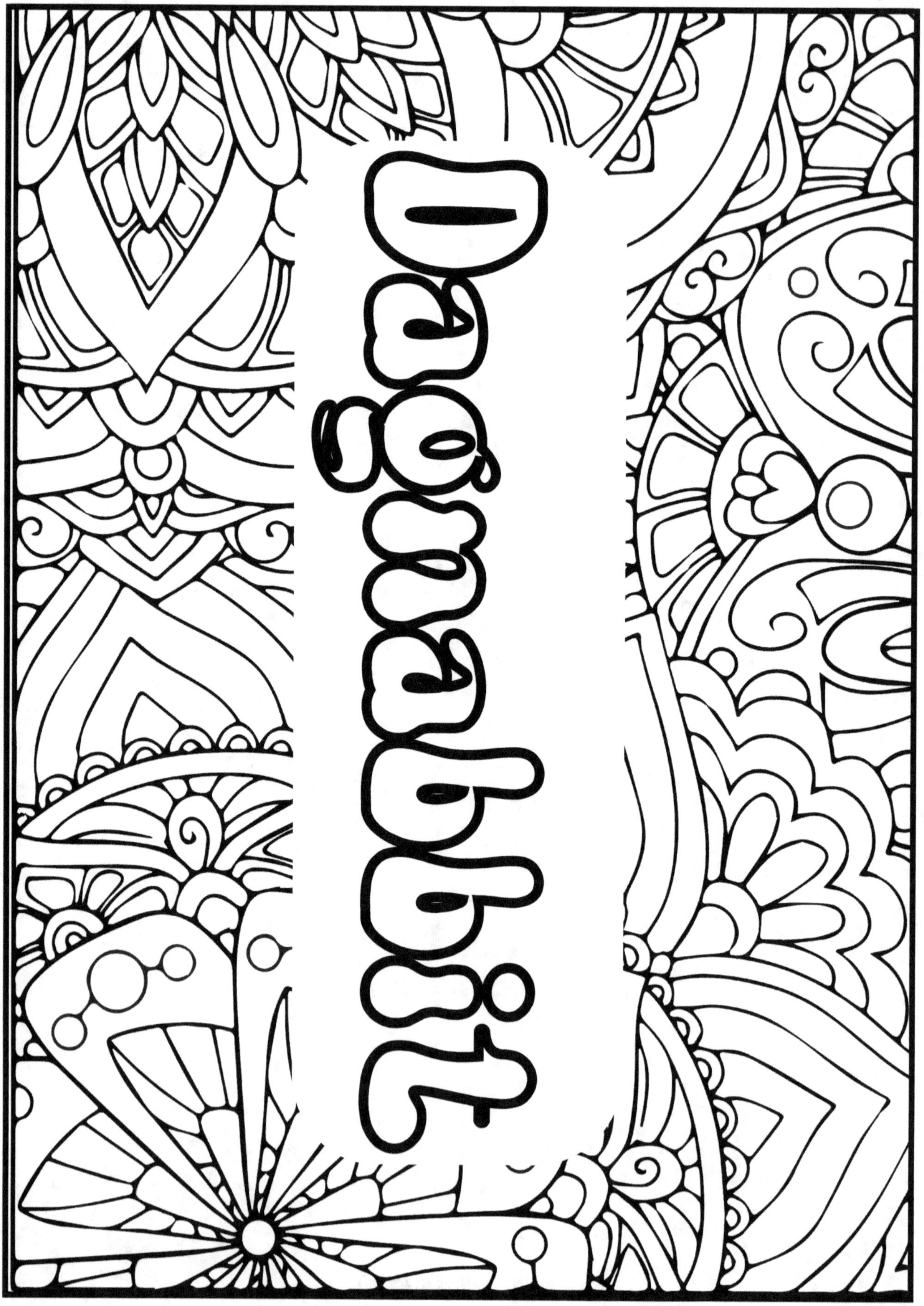
Dagnabbit

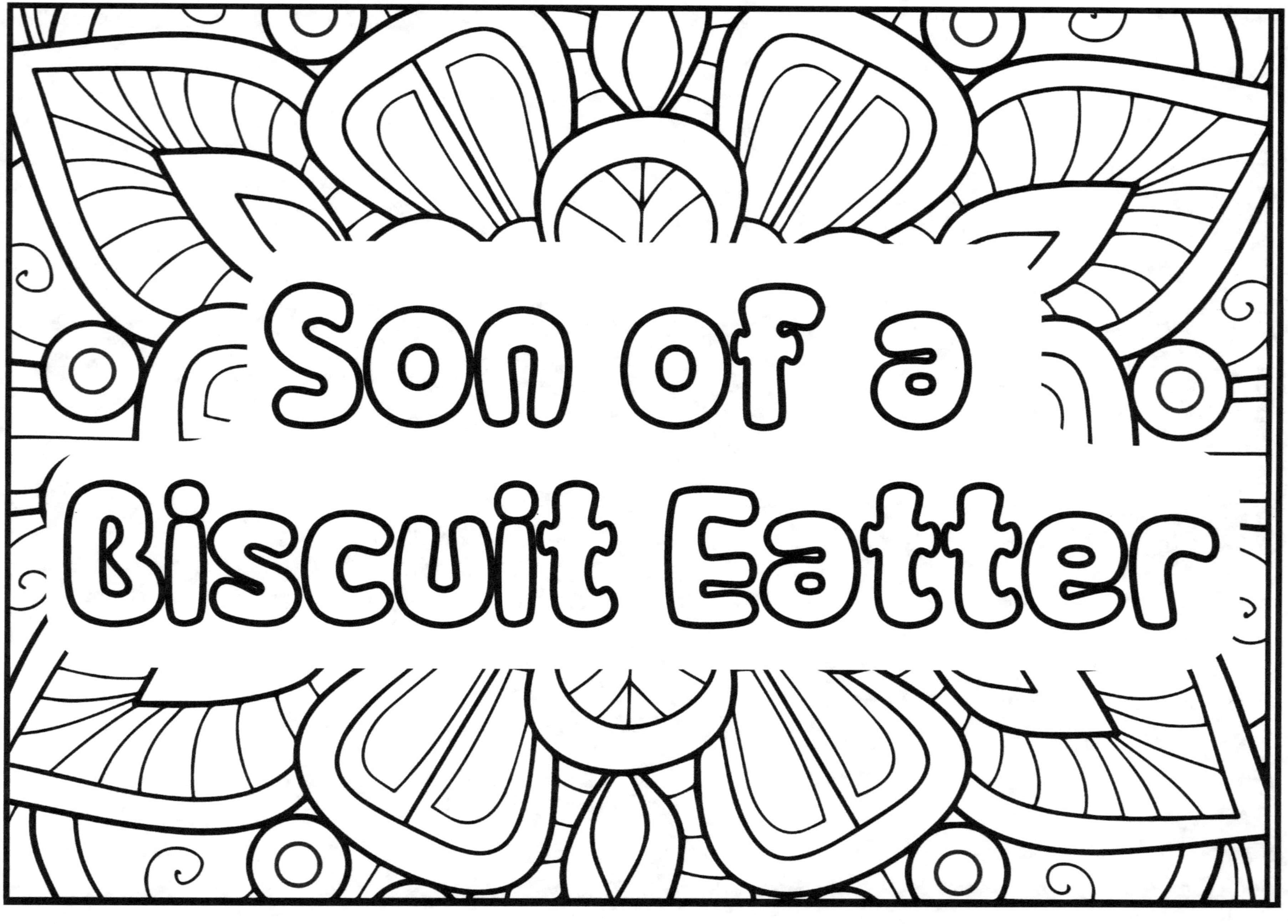
Son of a
Biscuit Eatter

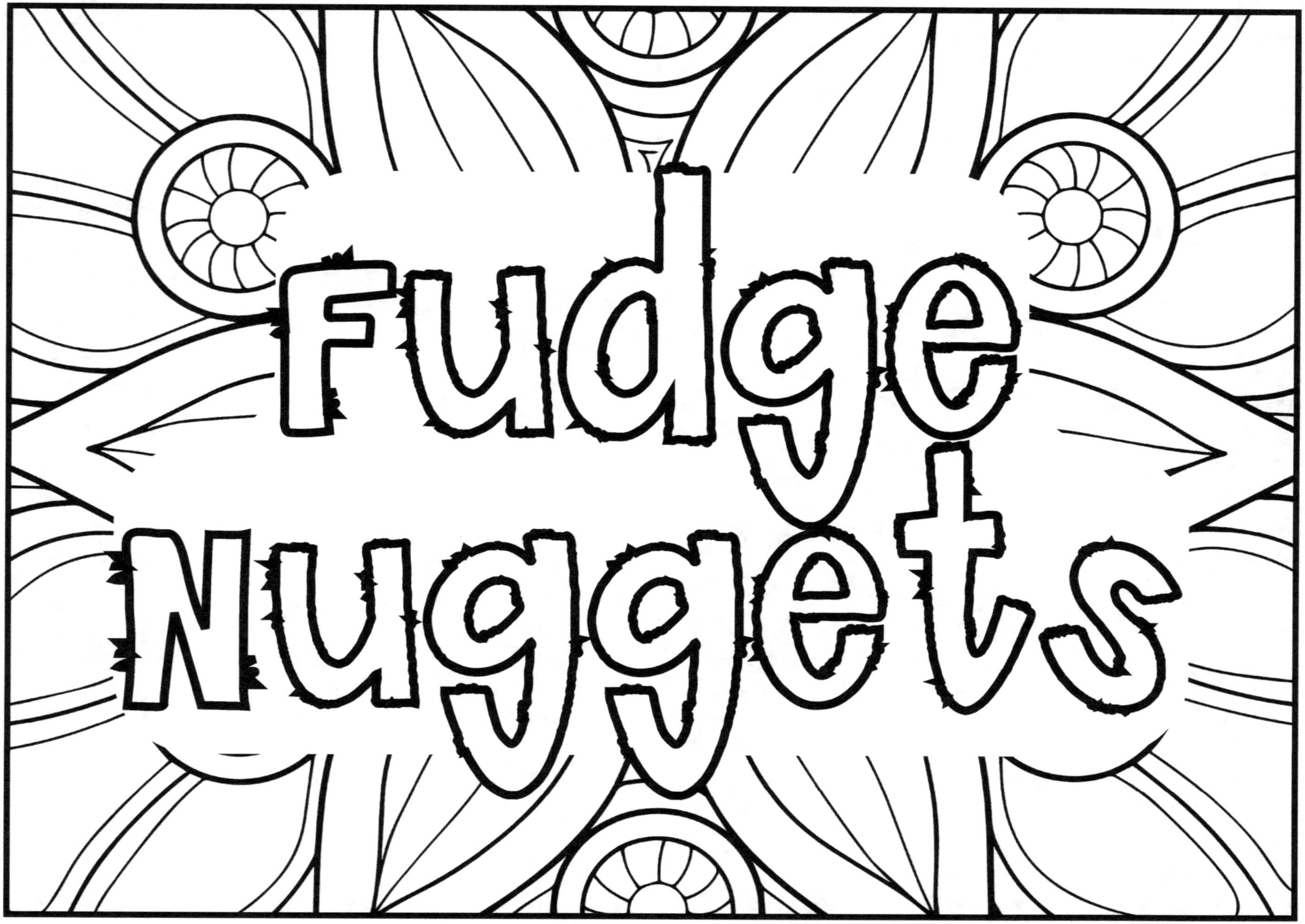
Fudge
Nuggets

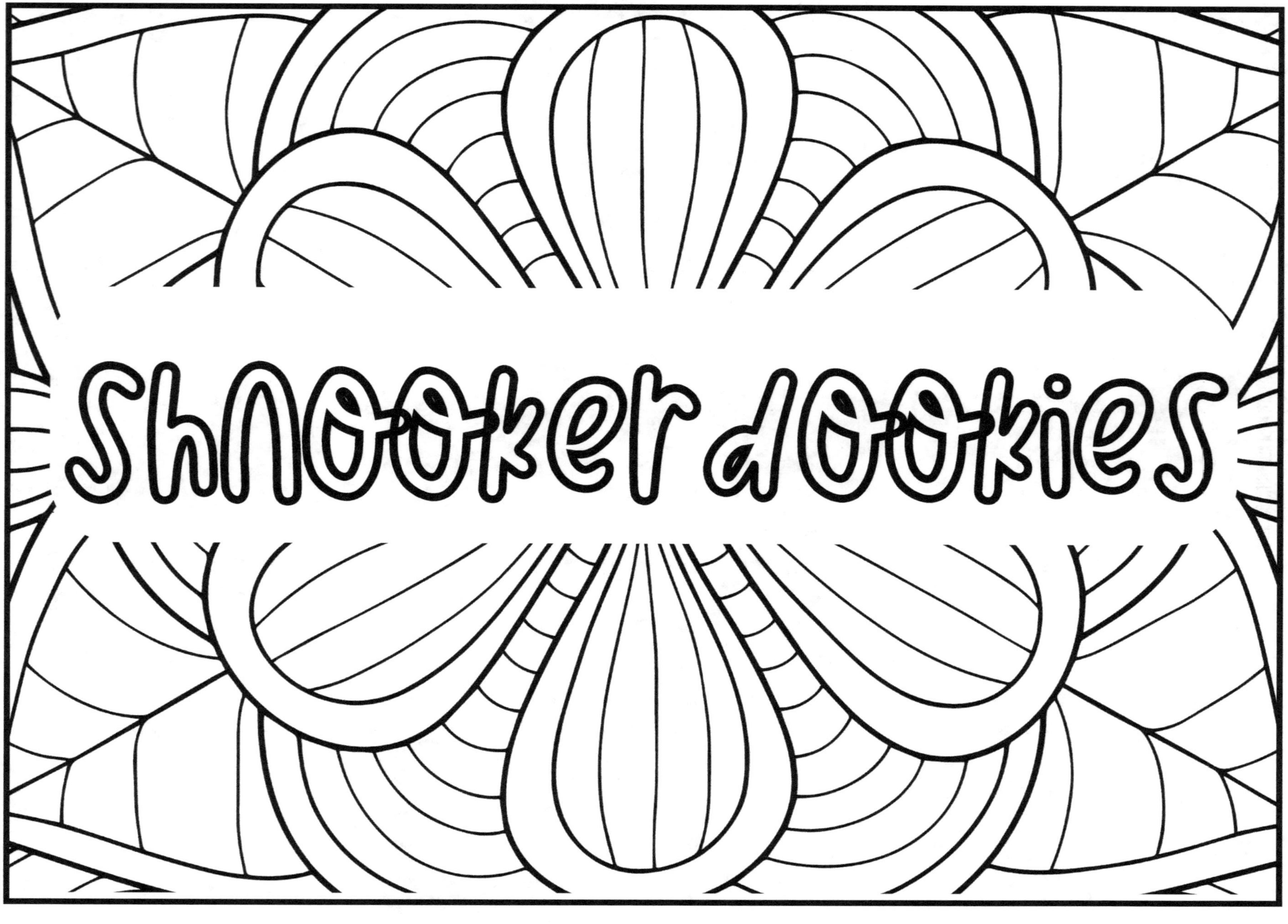
Shnooker dookies

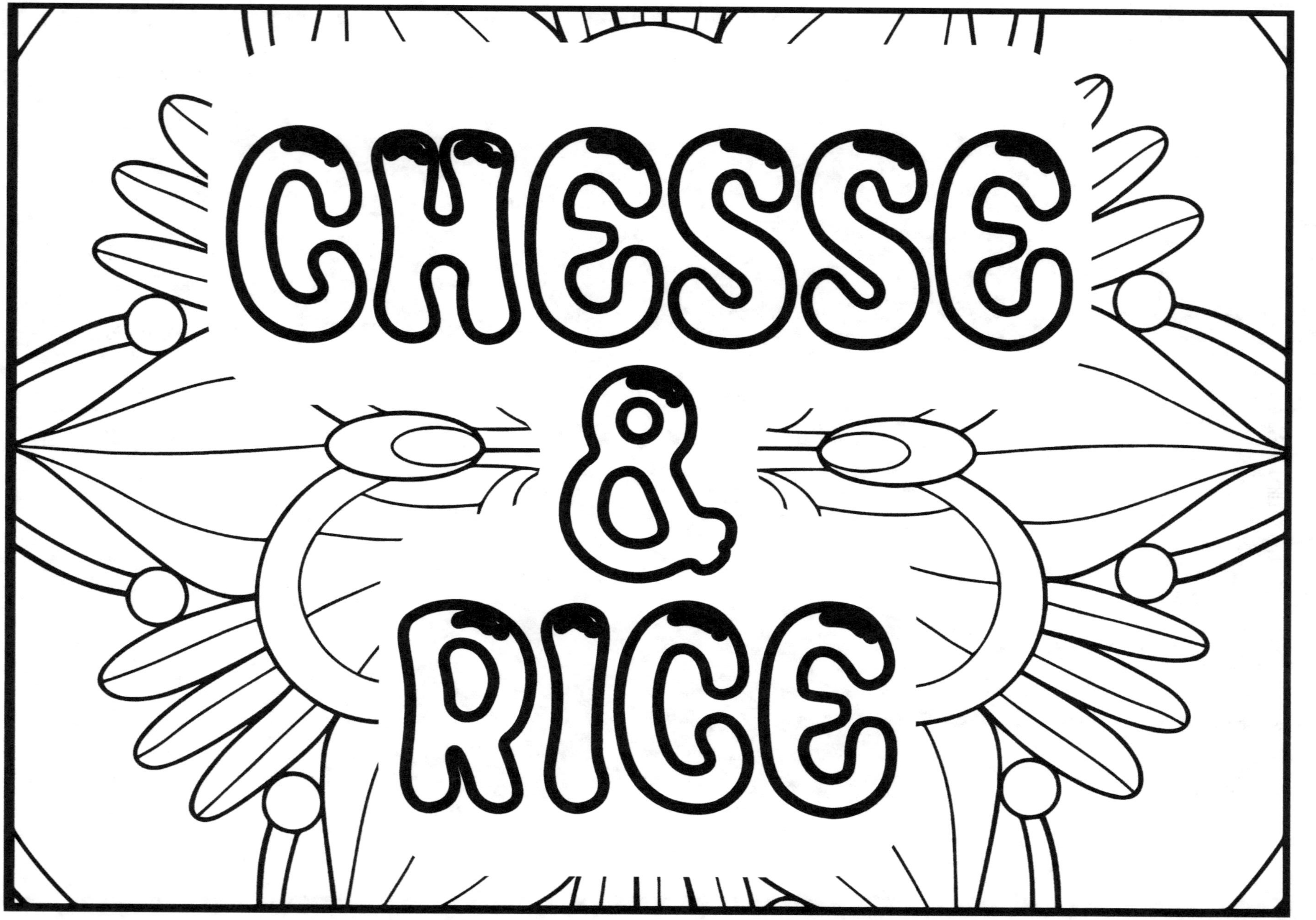
CHESSE
&
RICE

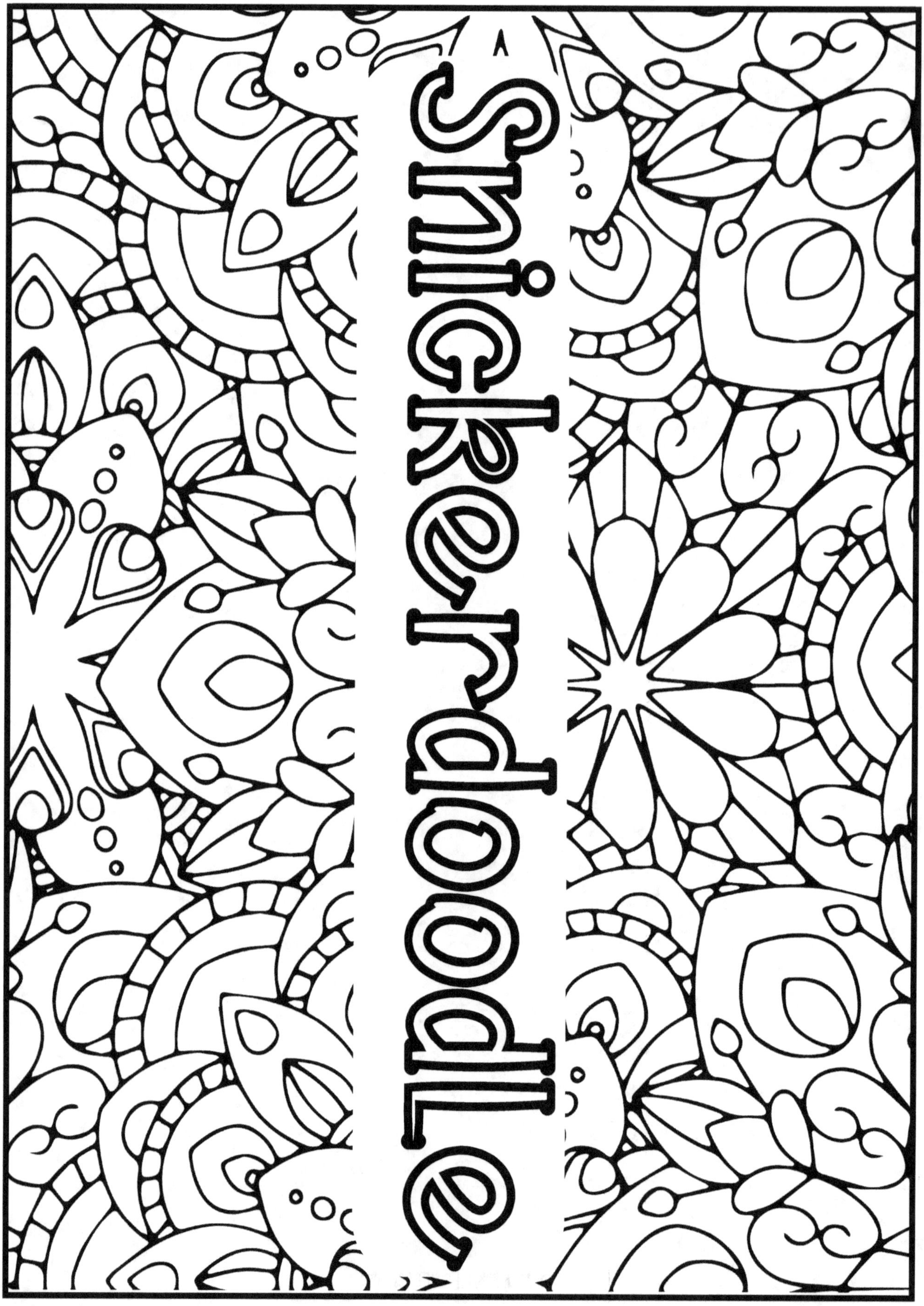
Snickerdoodle

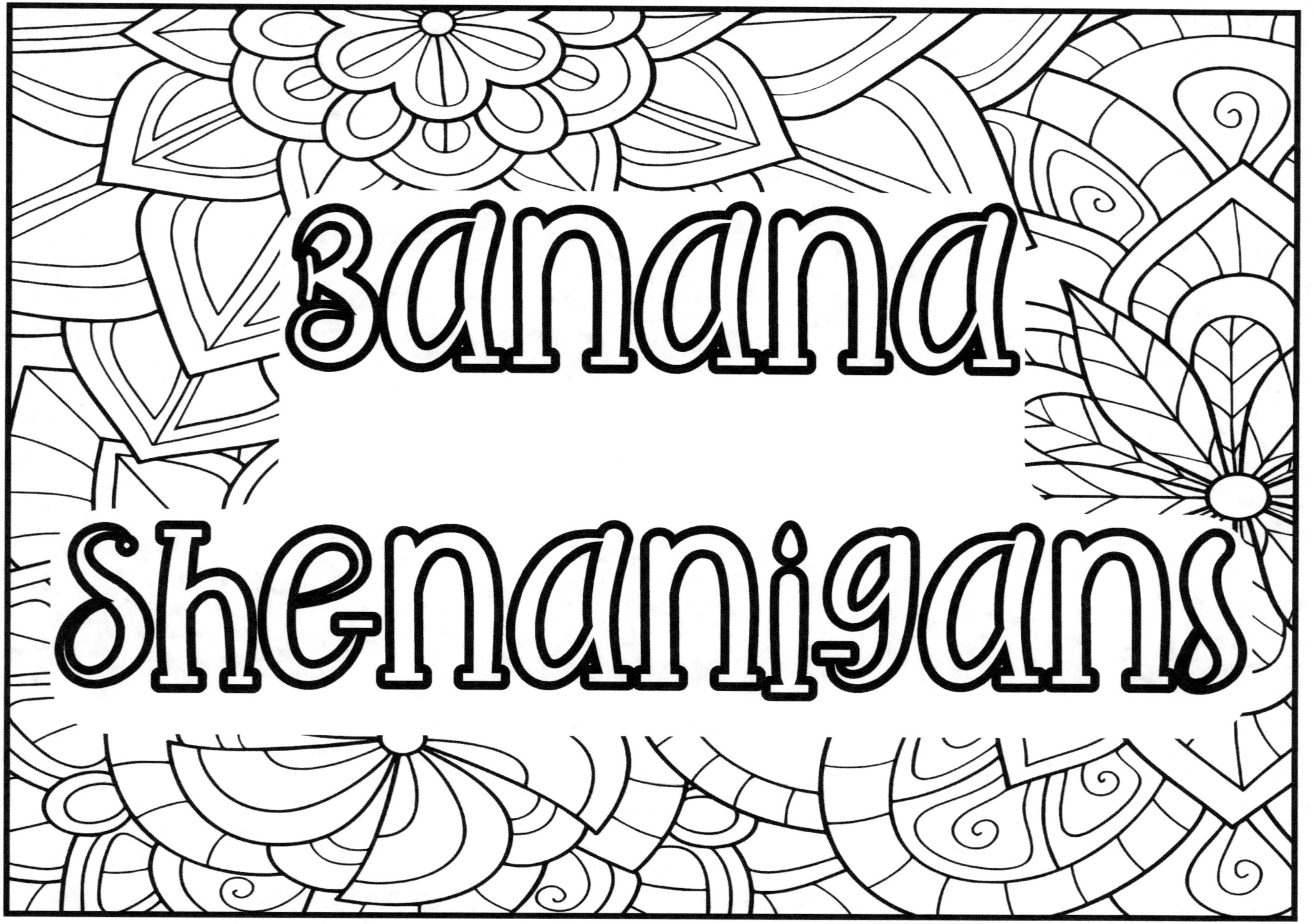
Banana
Shenanigans

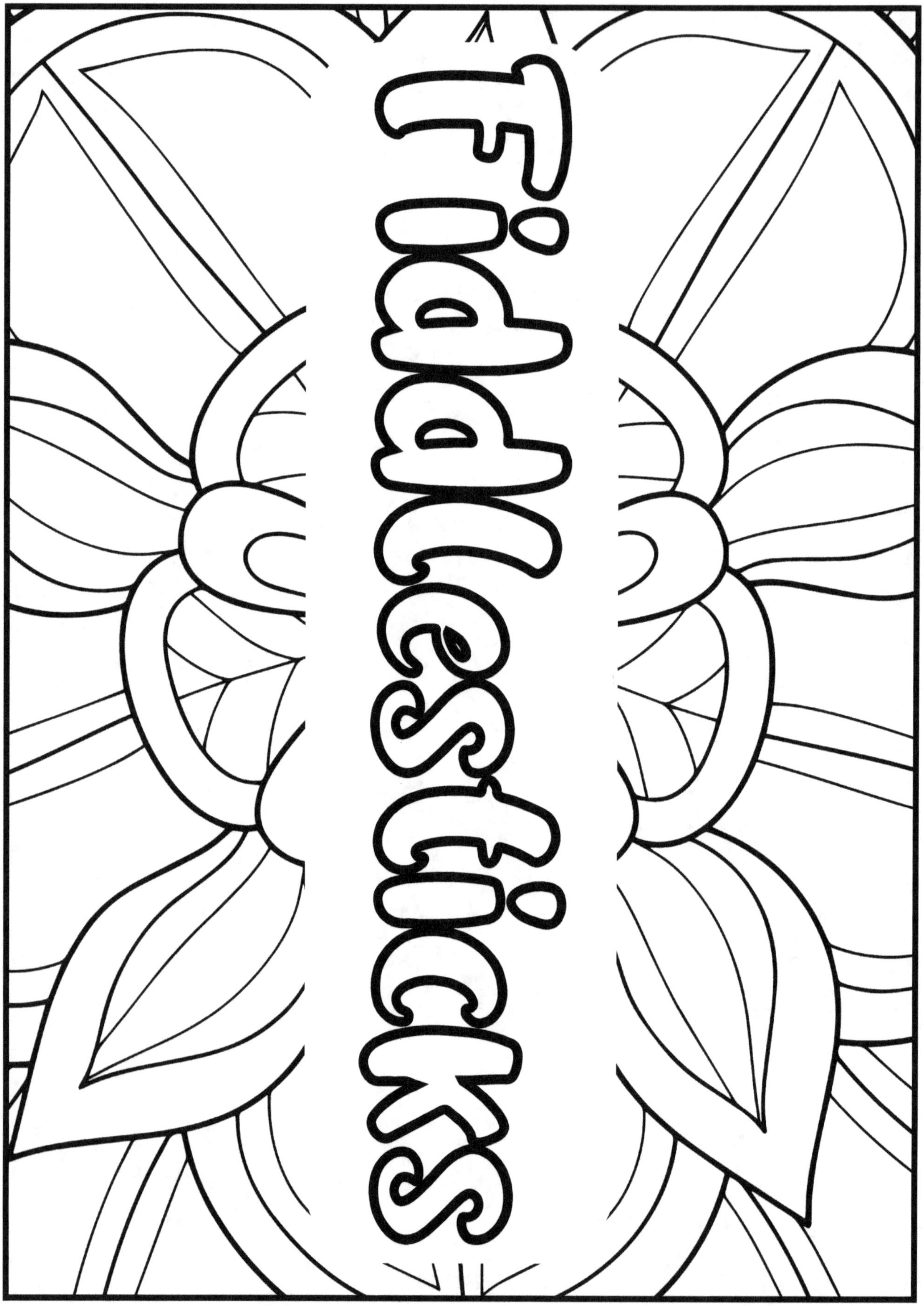
Fiddlesticks

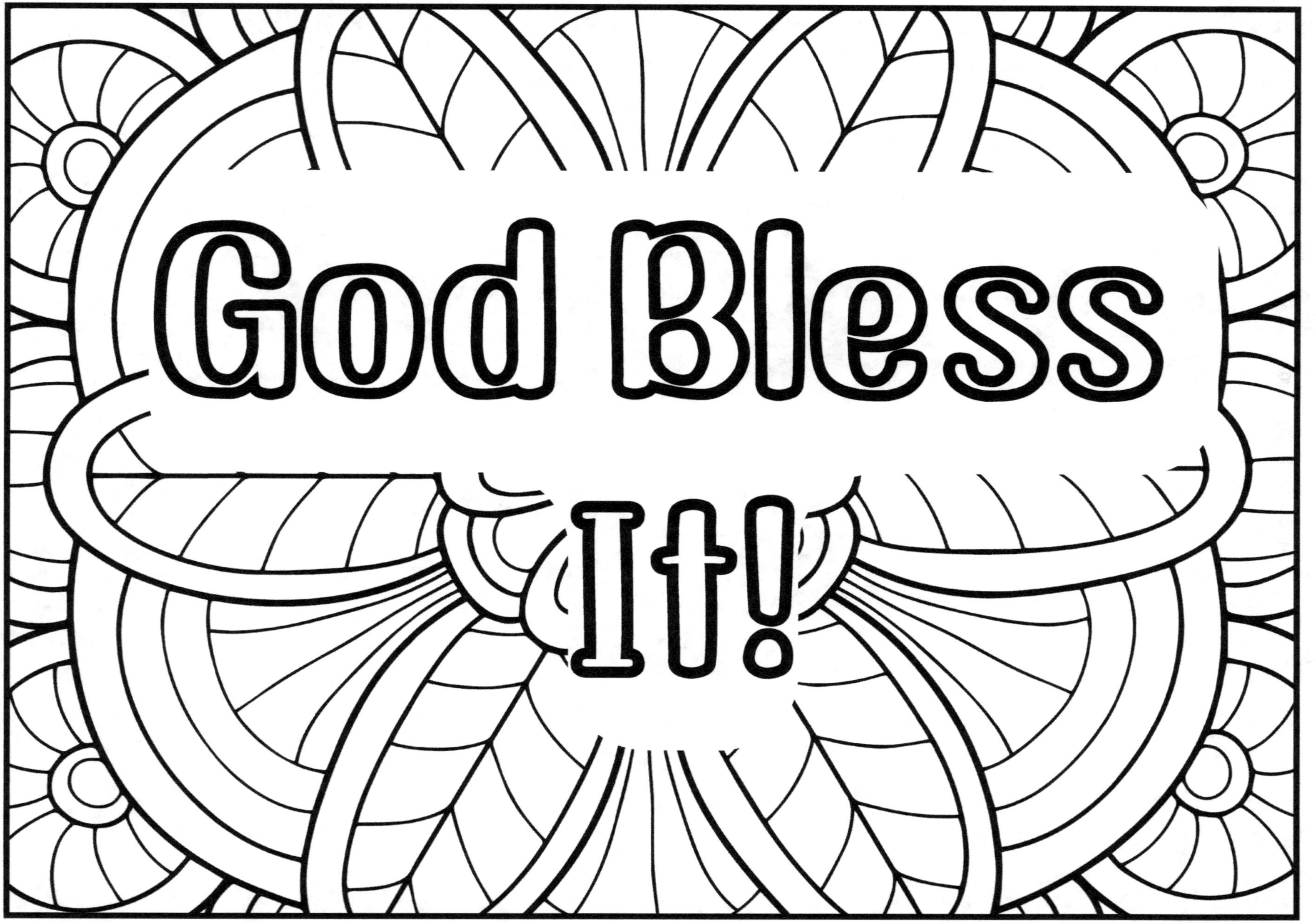
God Bless
It!

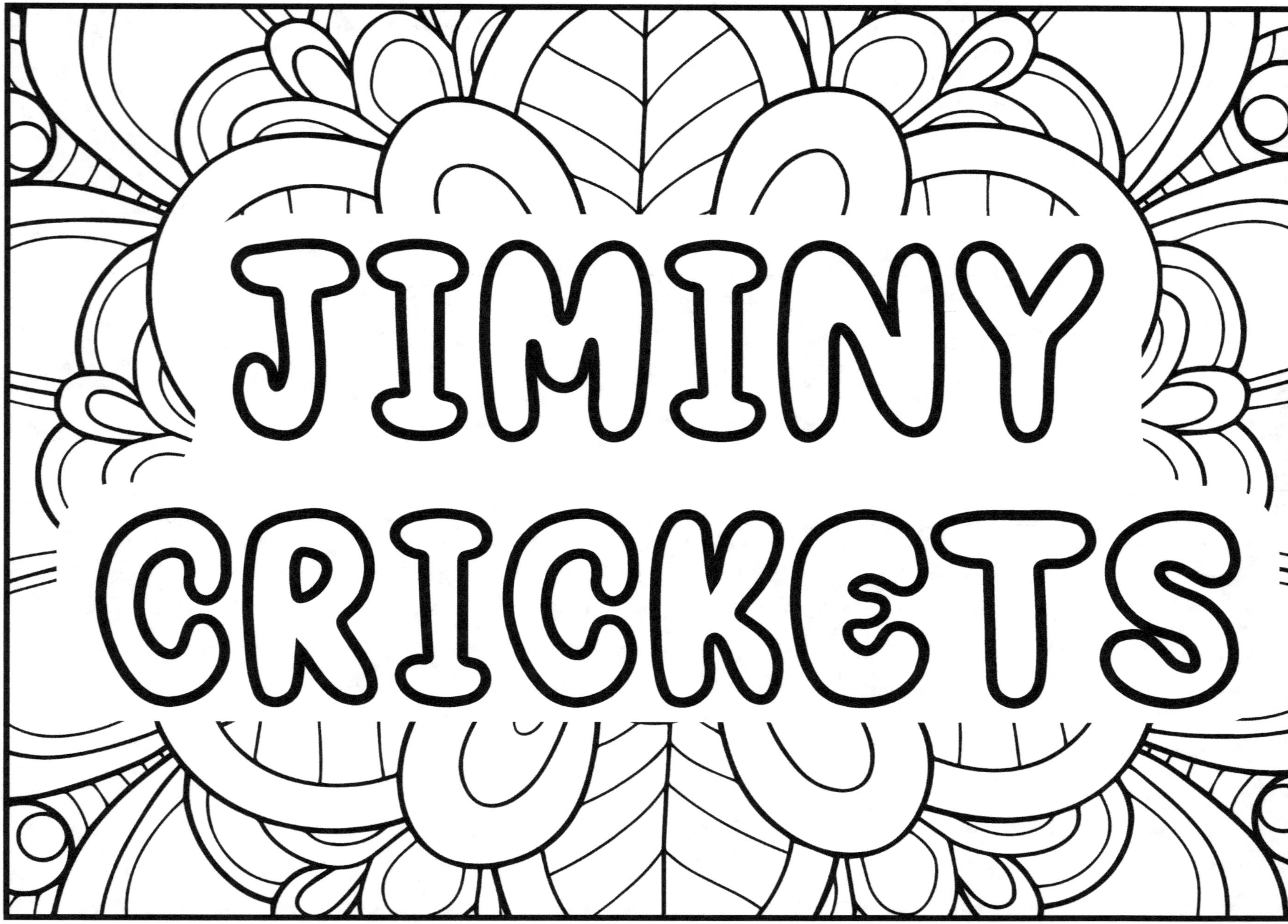
JIMINY
CRICKETS

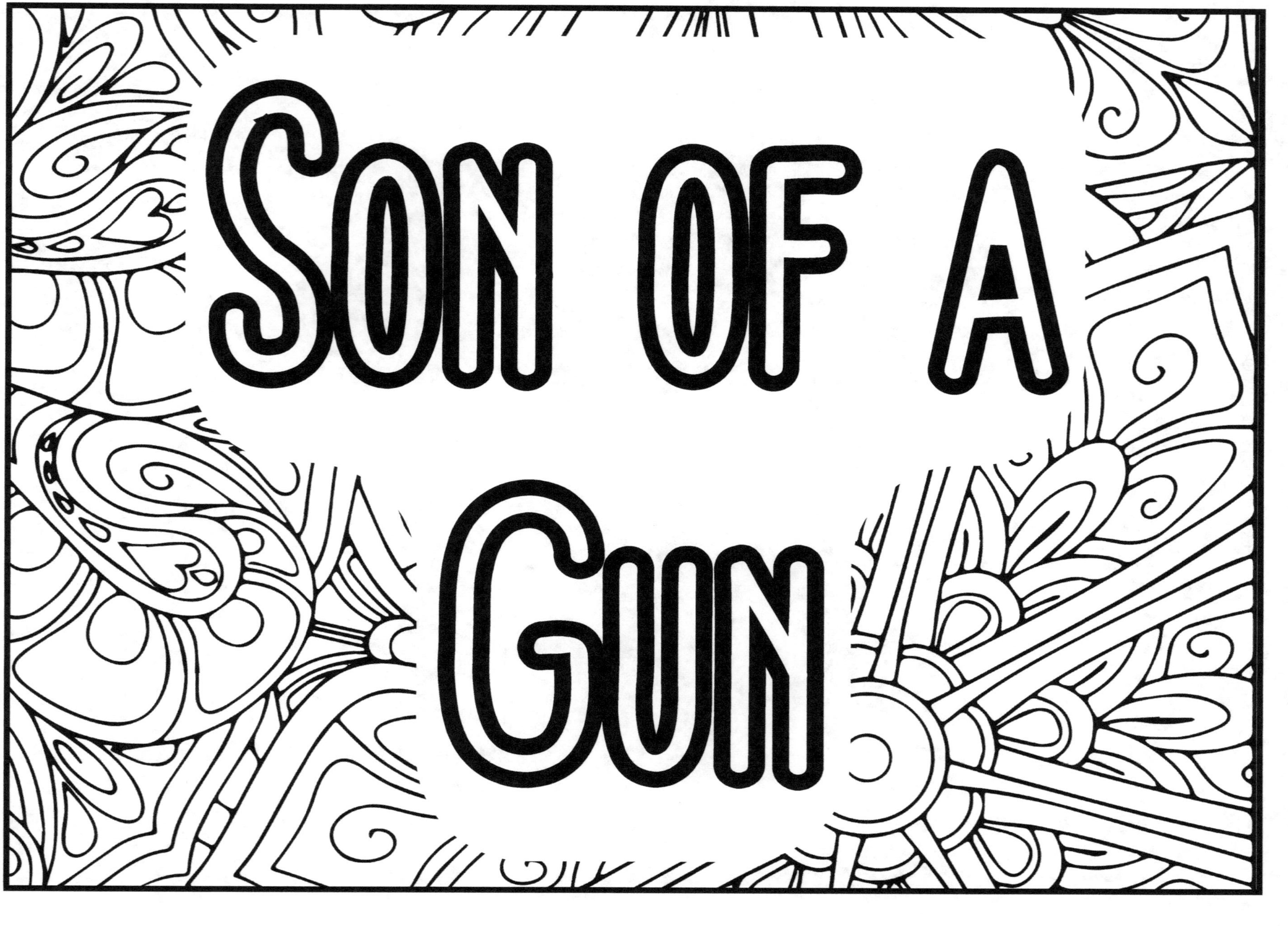
SON OF A
GUN

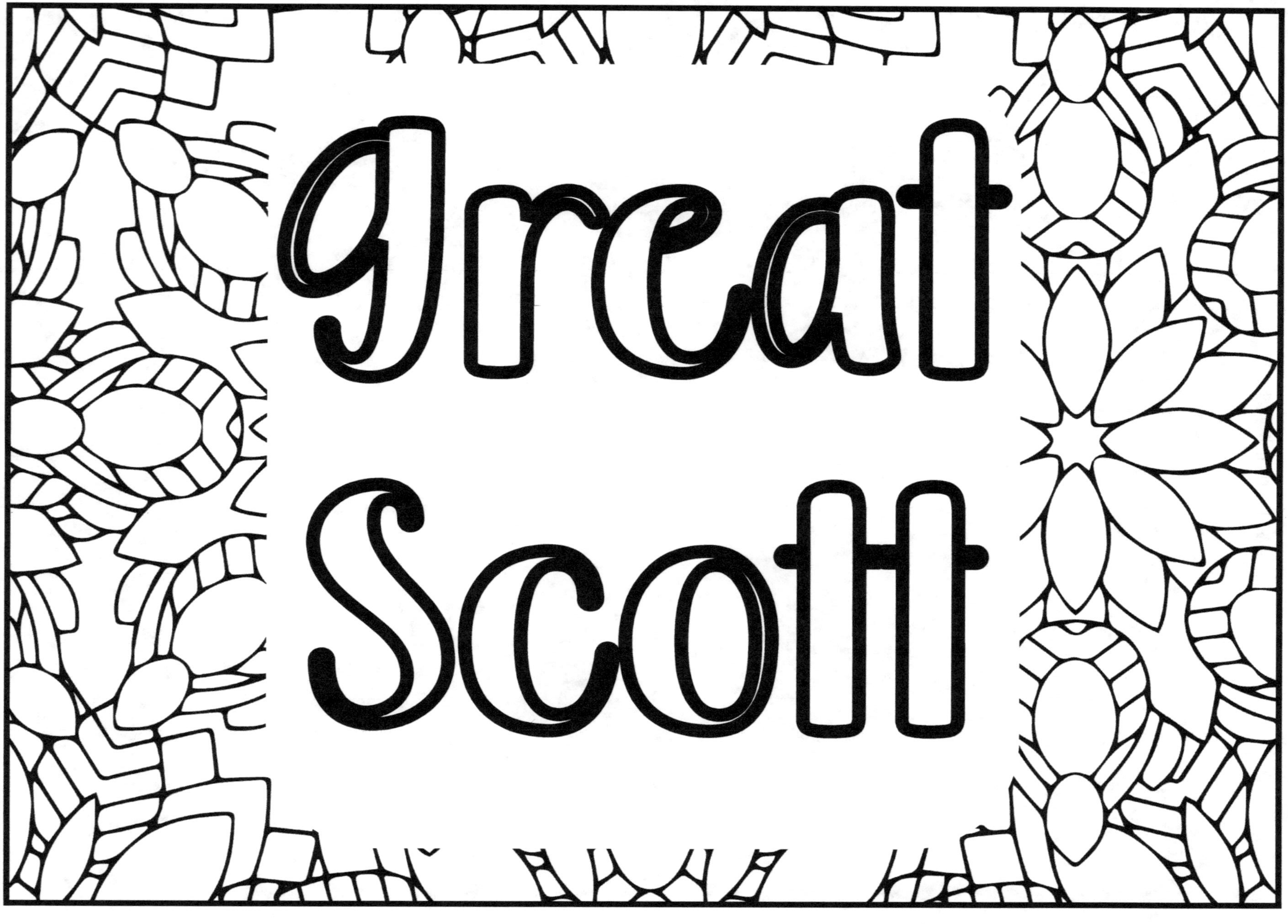
great
Scott

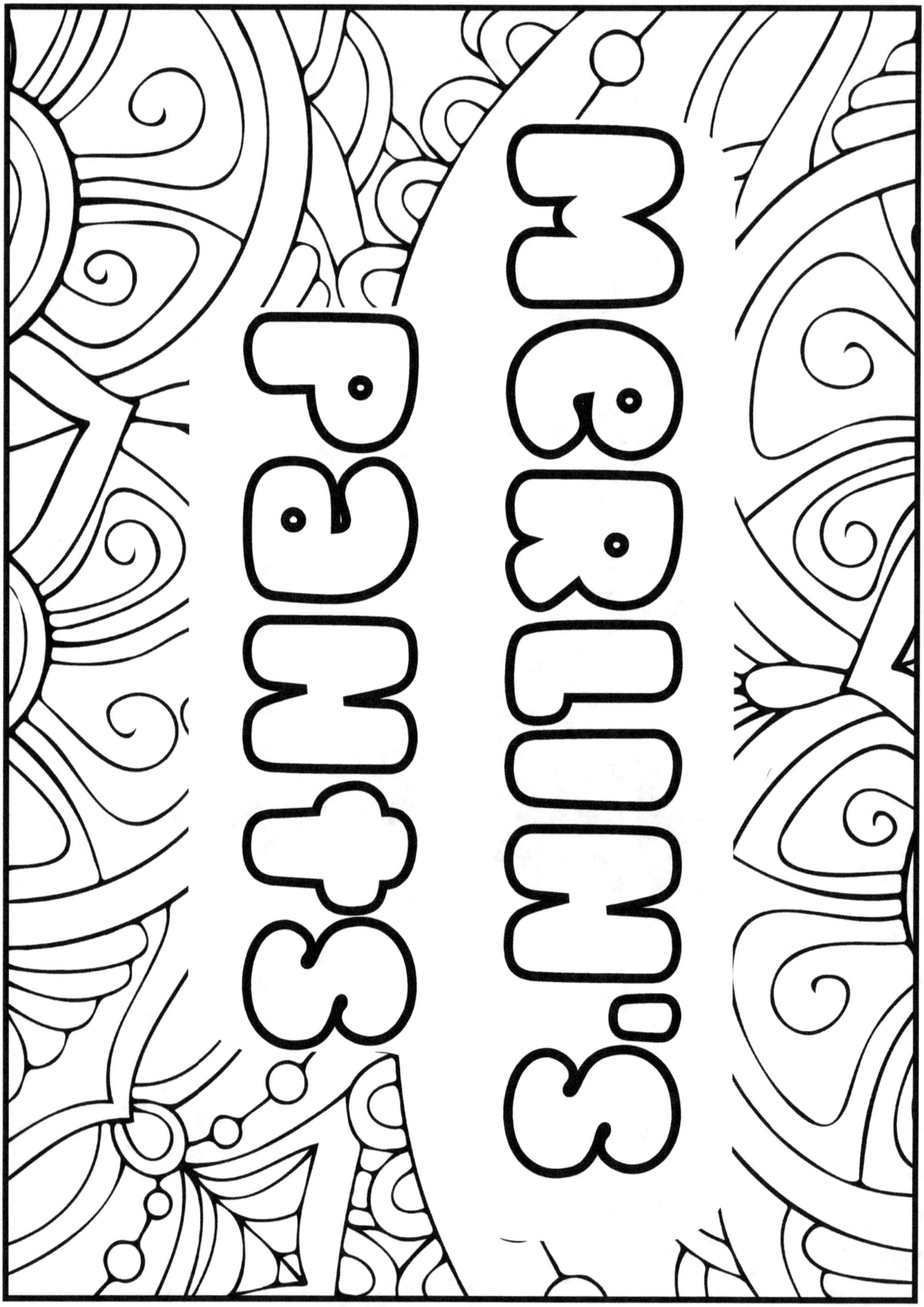
MERLIN'S
PANTS

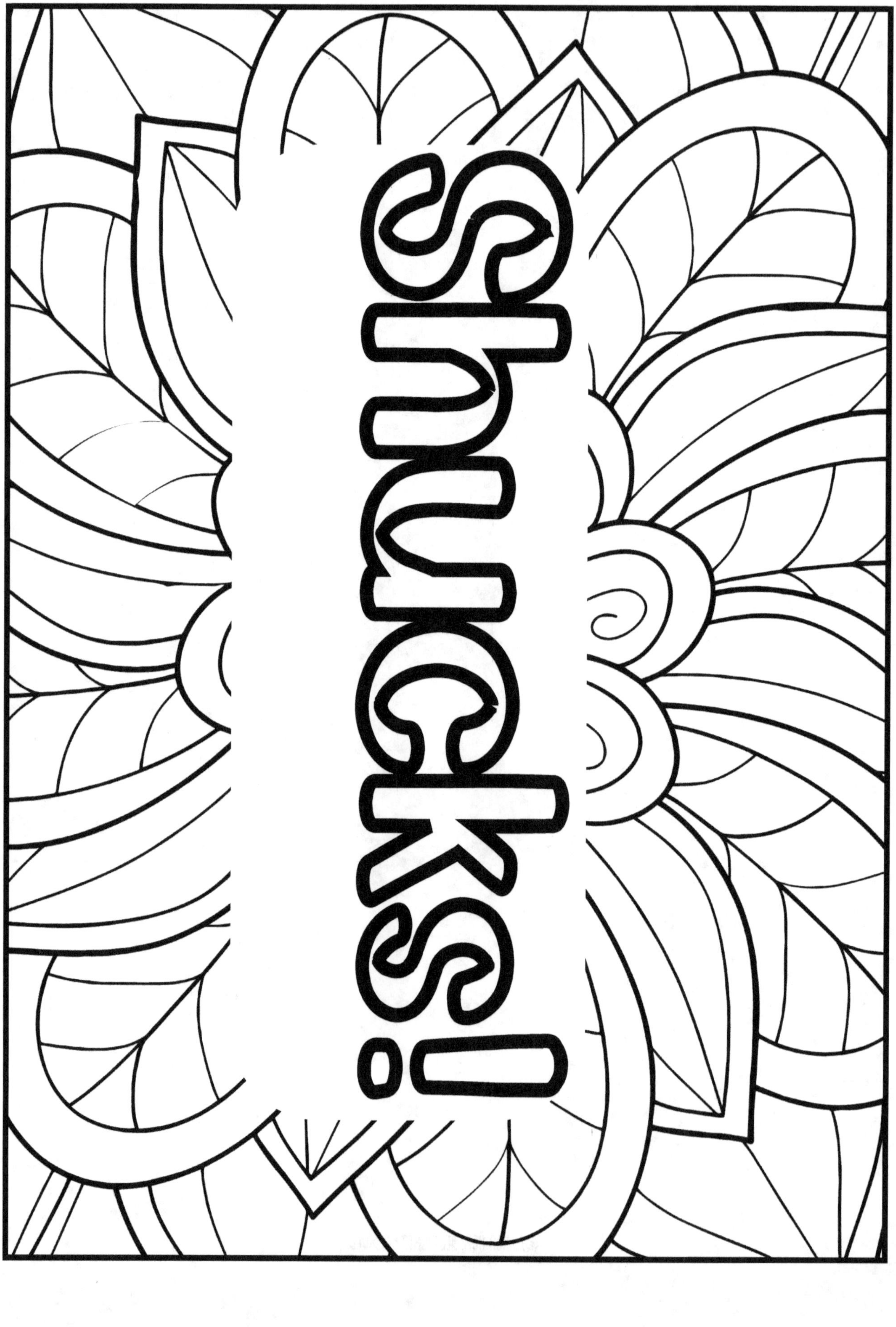
Shucks!

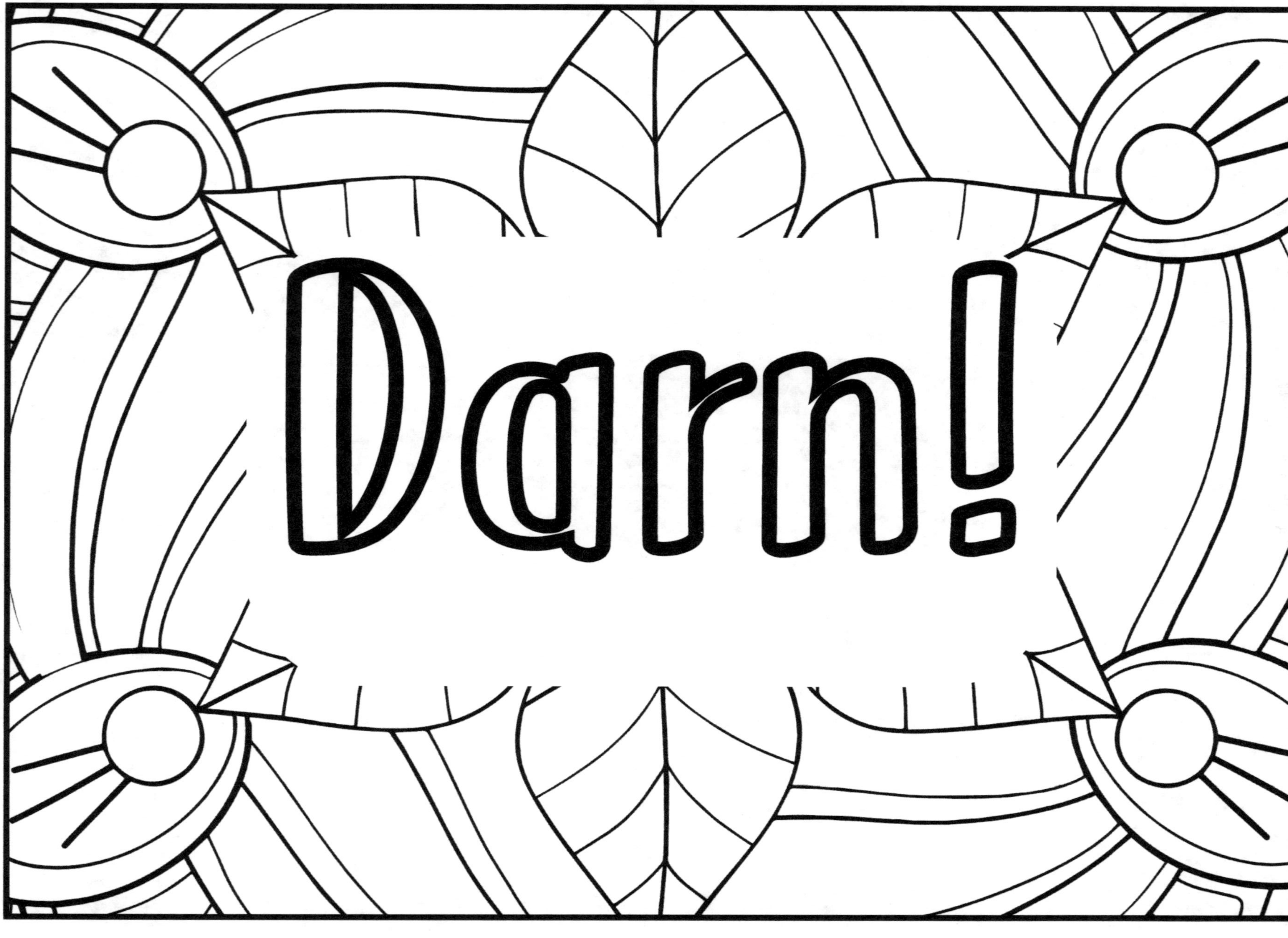
Darn!

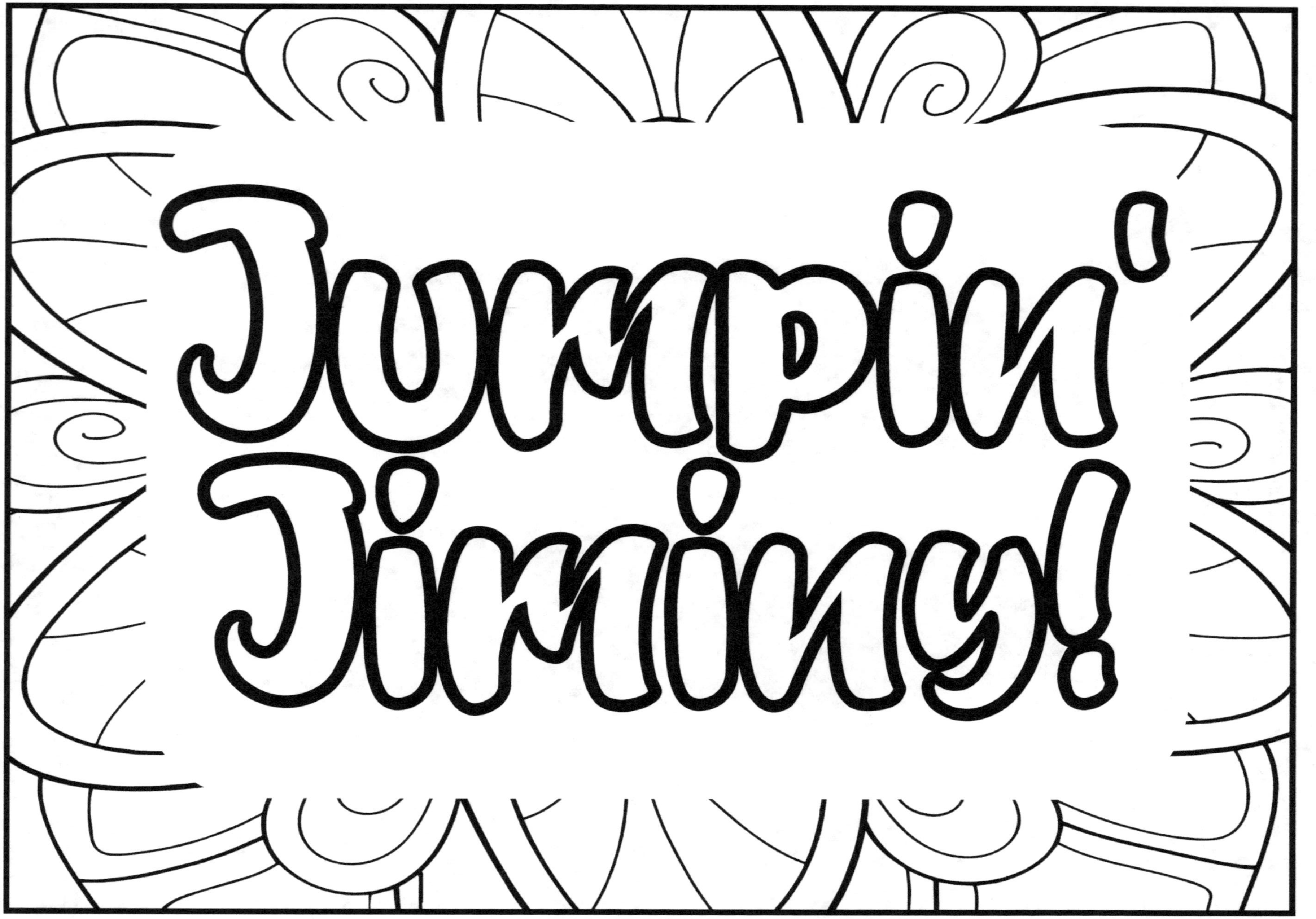
Jumpin'
Jiminy!

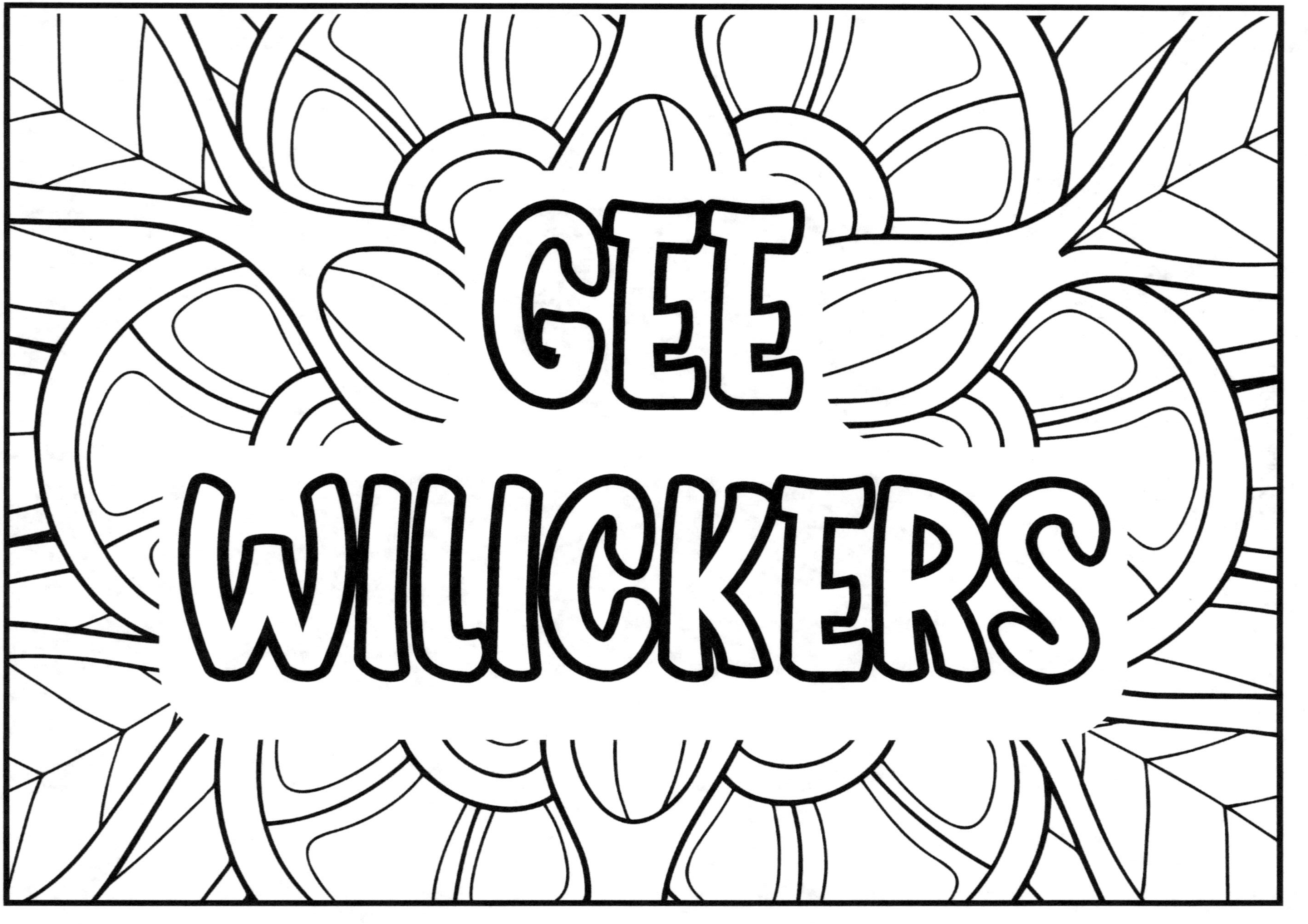
GEE
WILICKERS

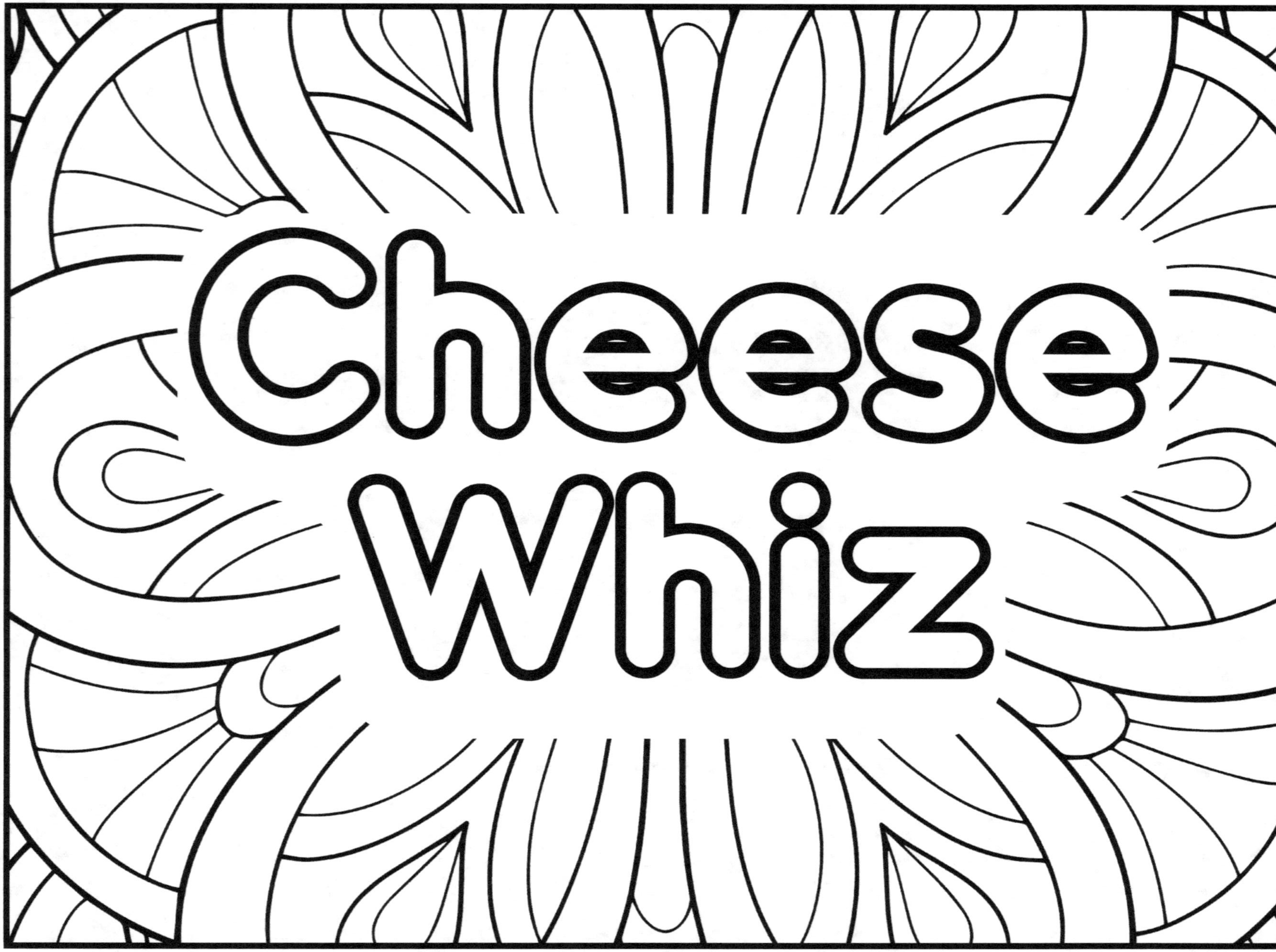
Cheese
Whiz

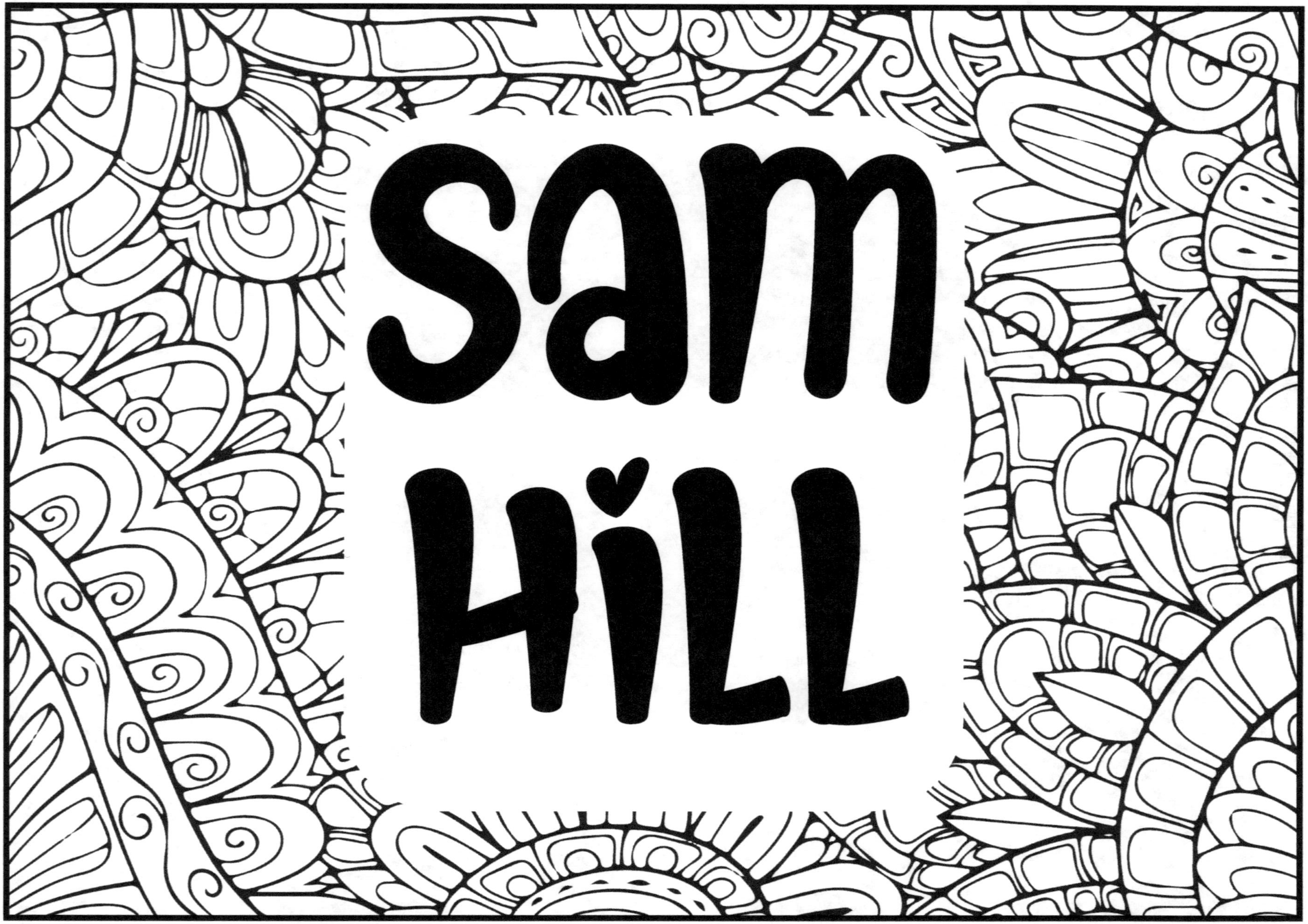
Sam
Hill

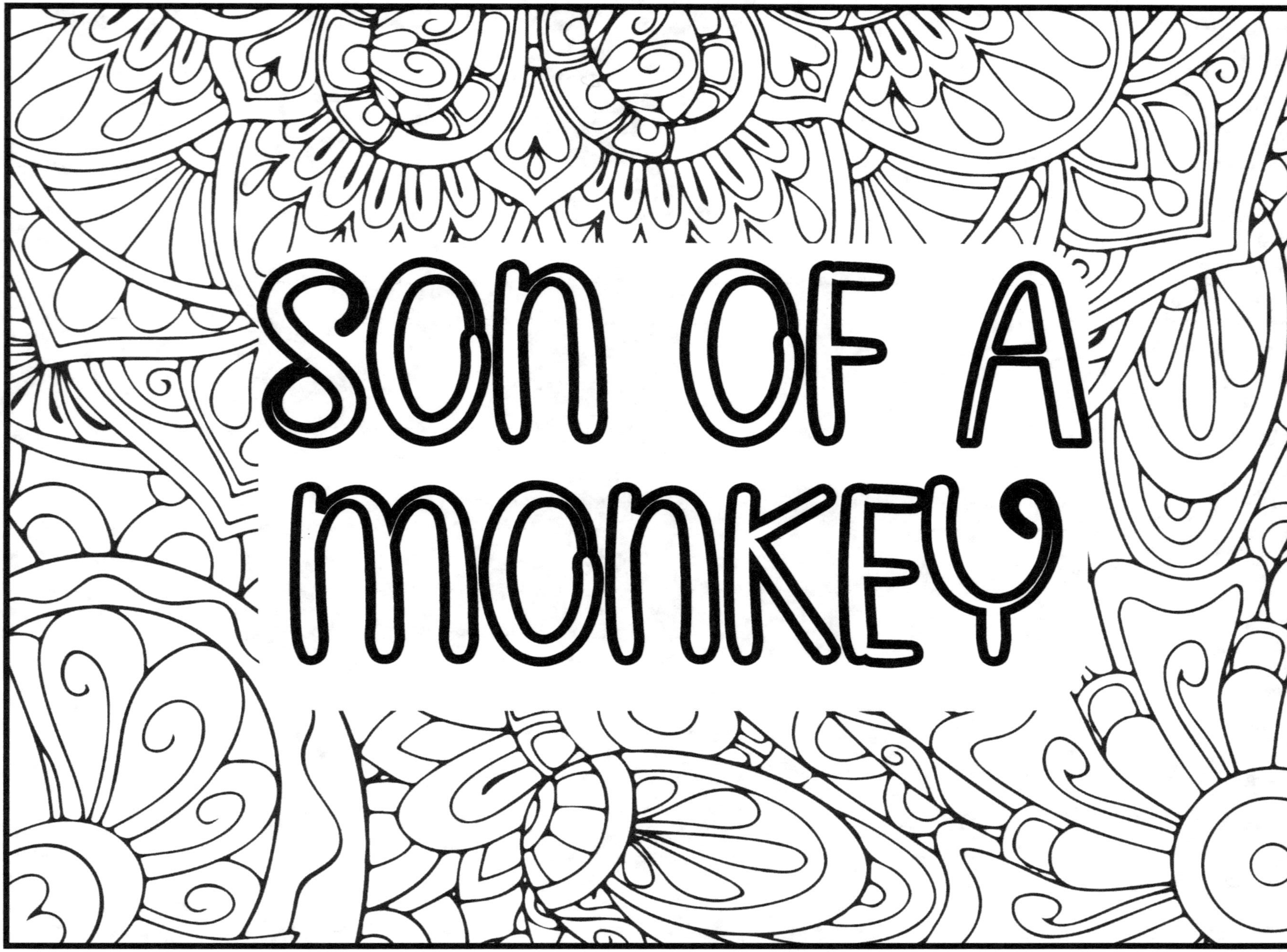
SON OF A
MONKEY

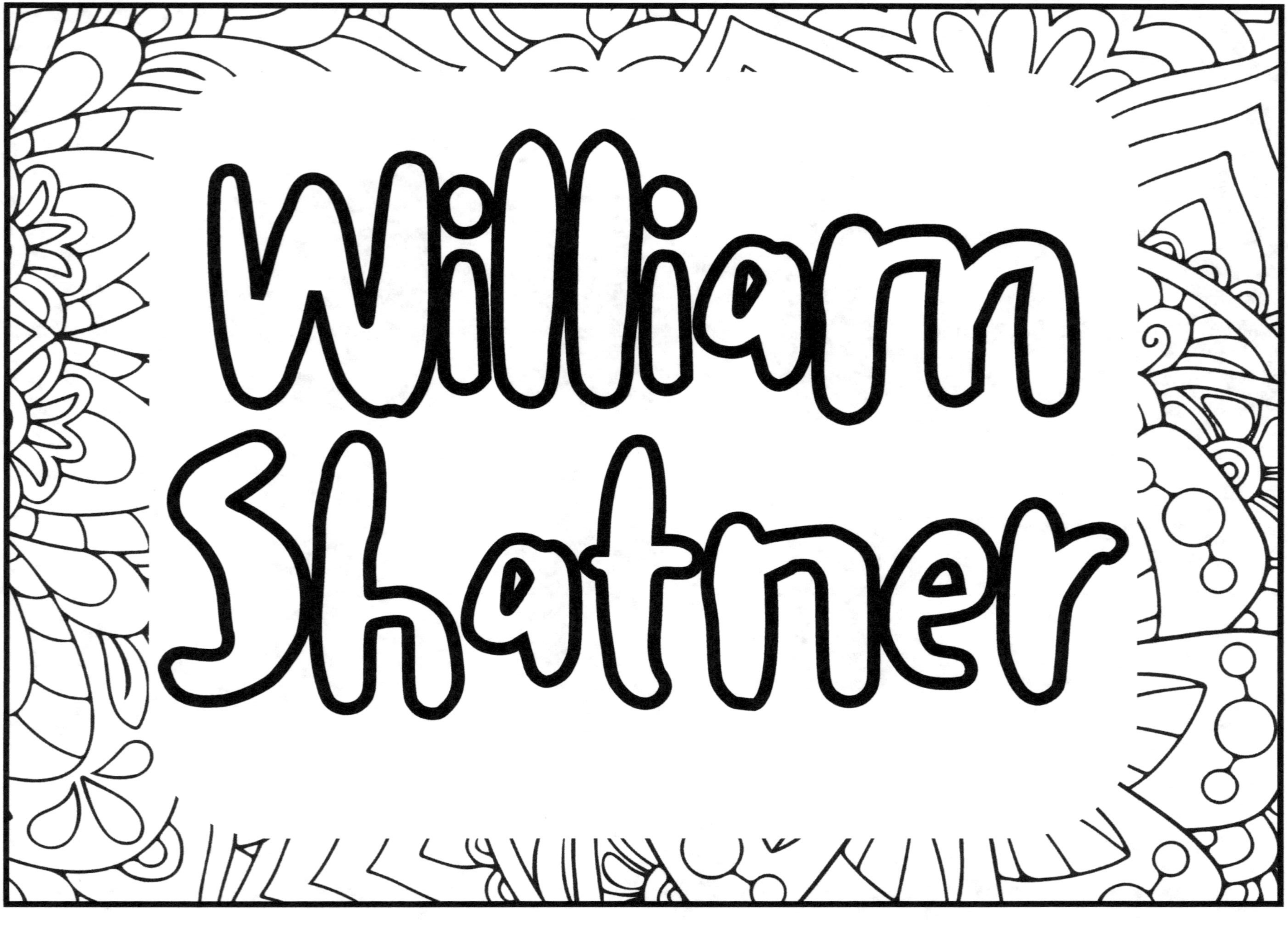
William
Shatner

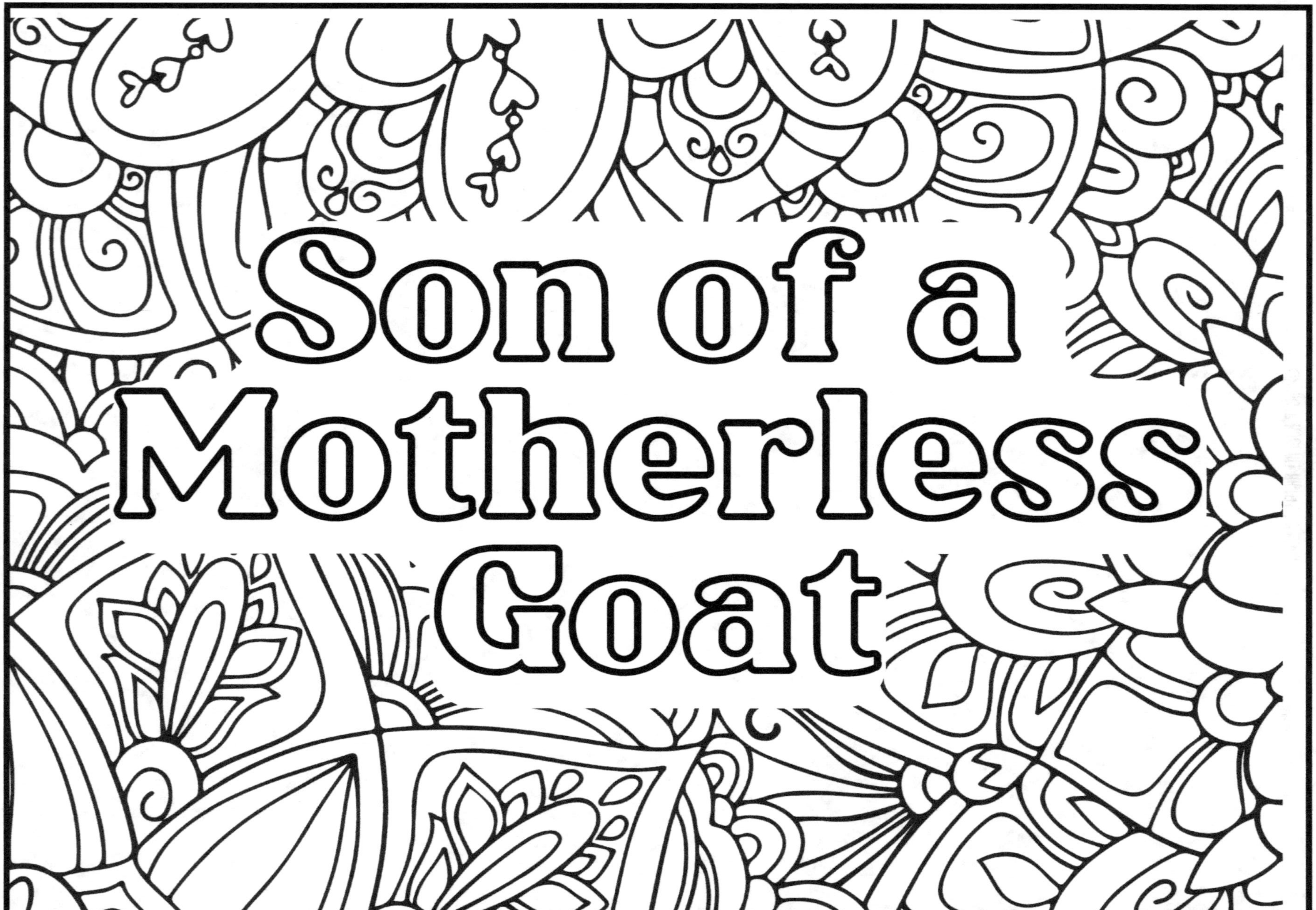
Son of a
Motherless
Goat

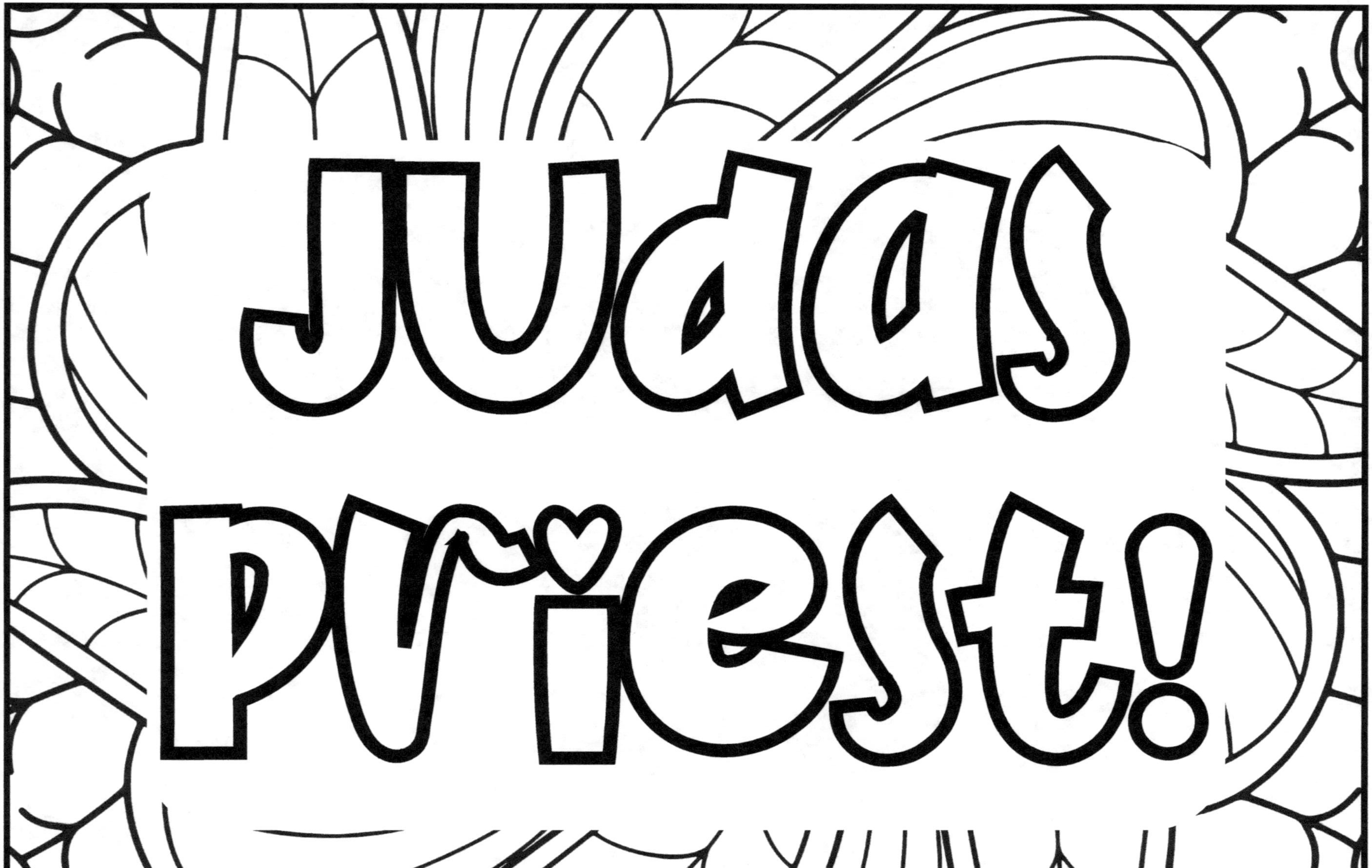
Judas
Priest!

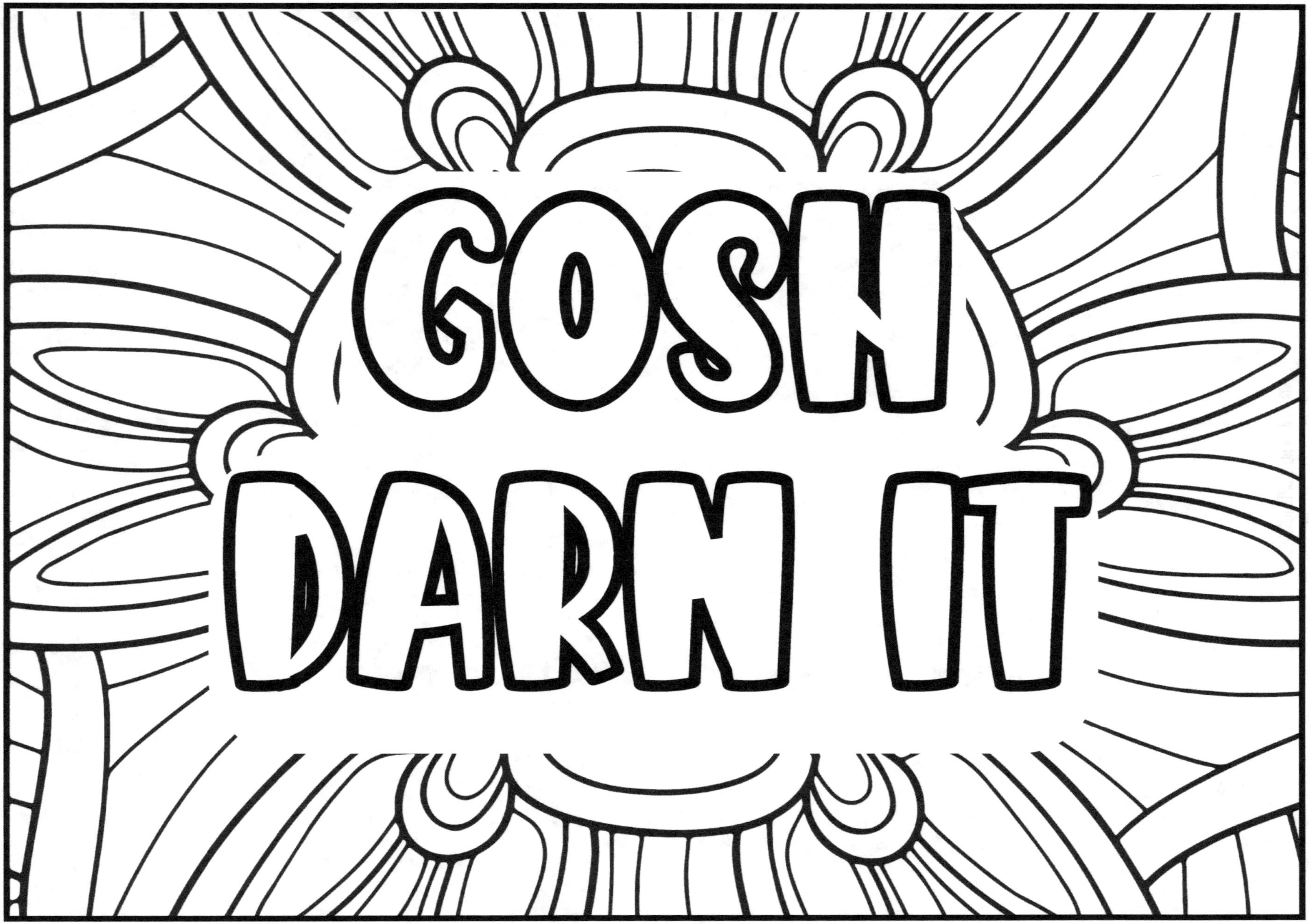
GOSH
DARN IT

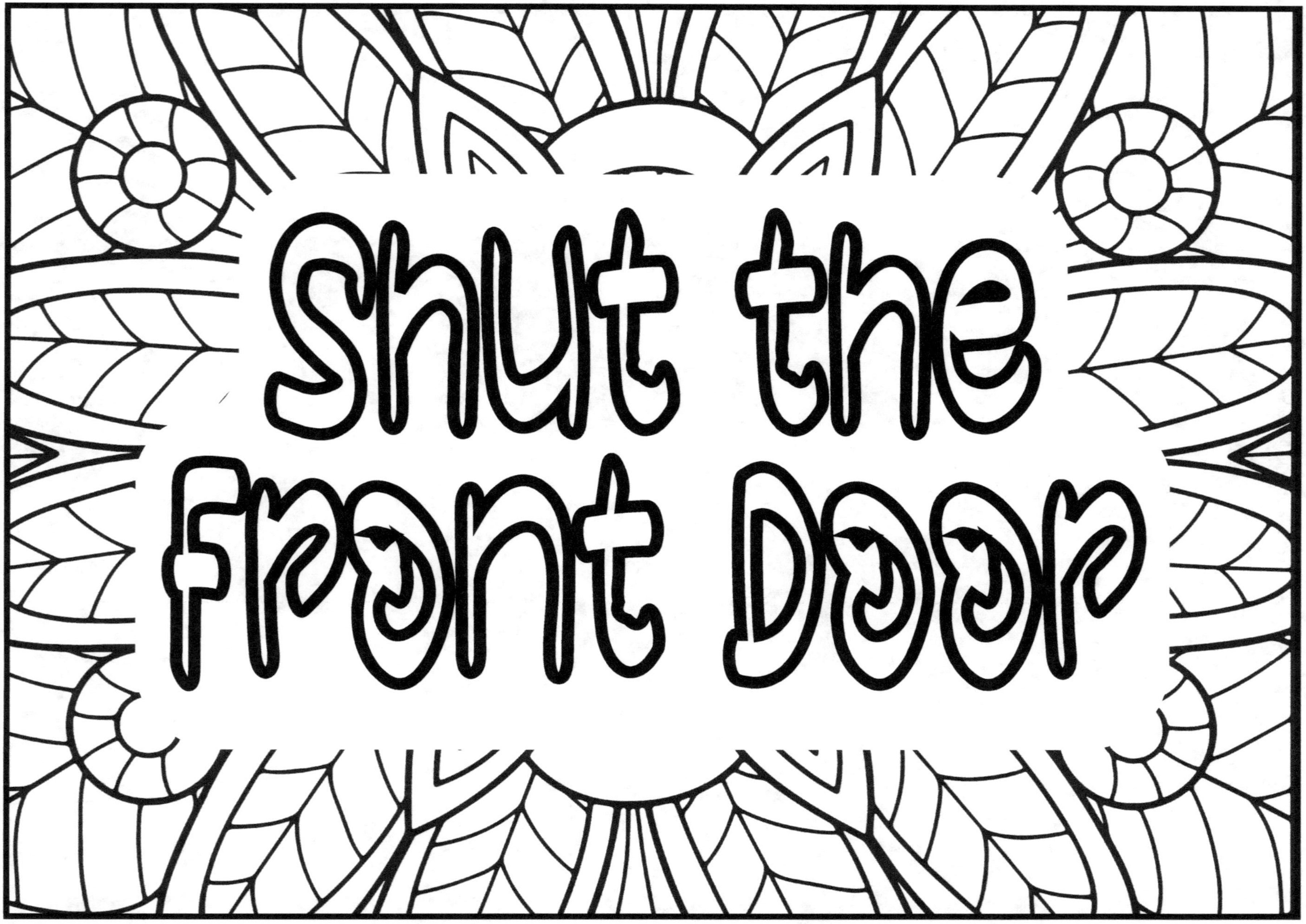
Shut the
Front Door

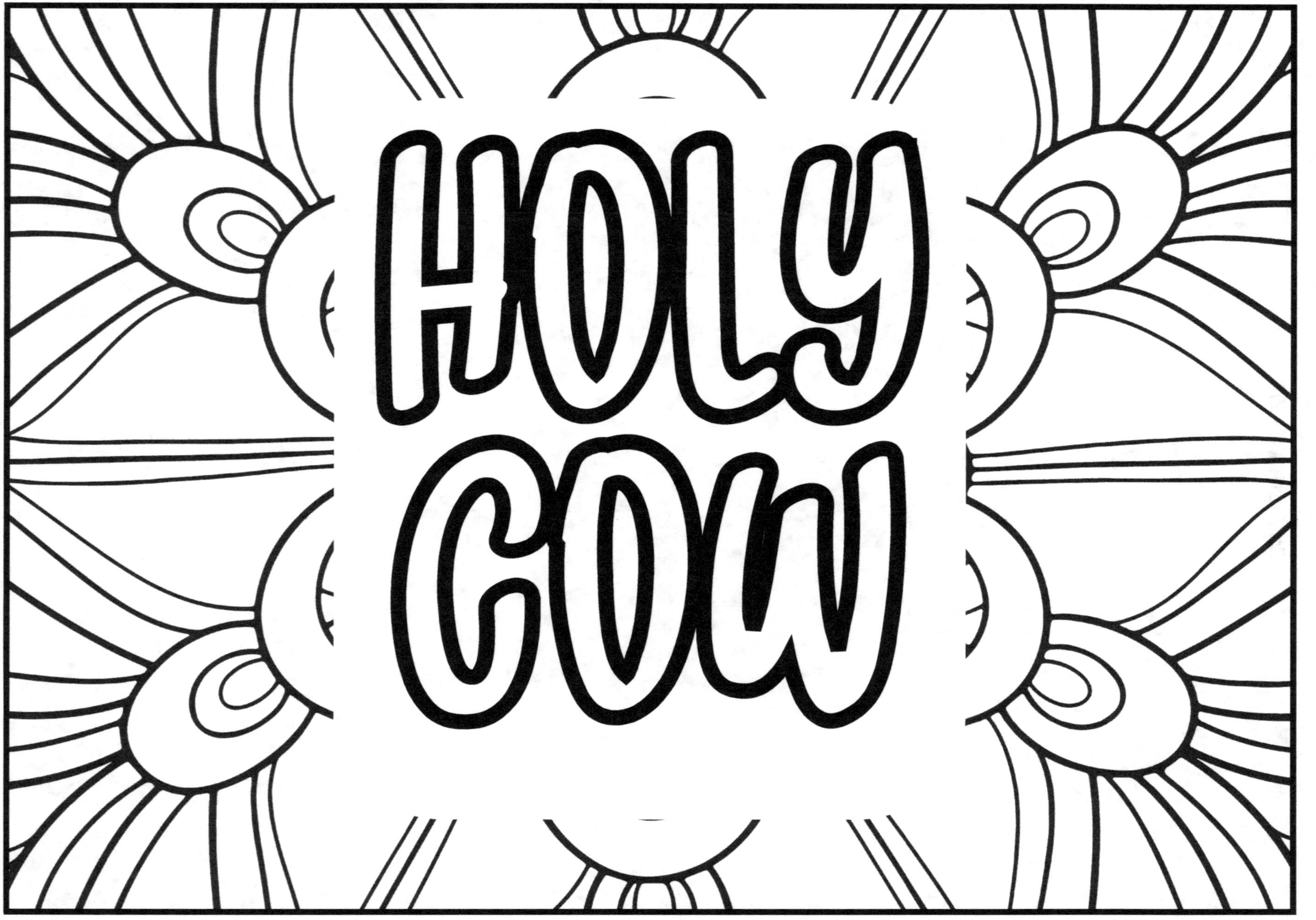
HOLY
COW

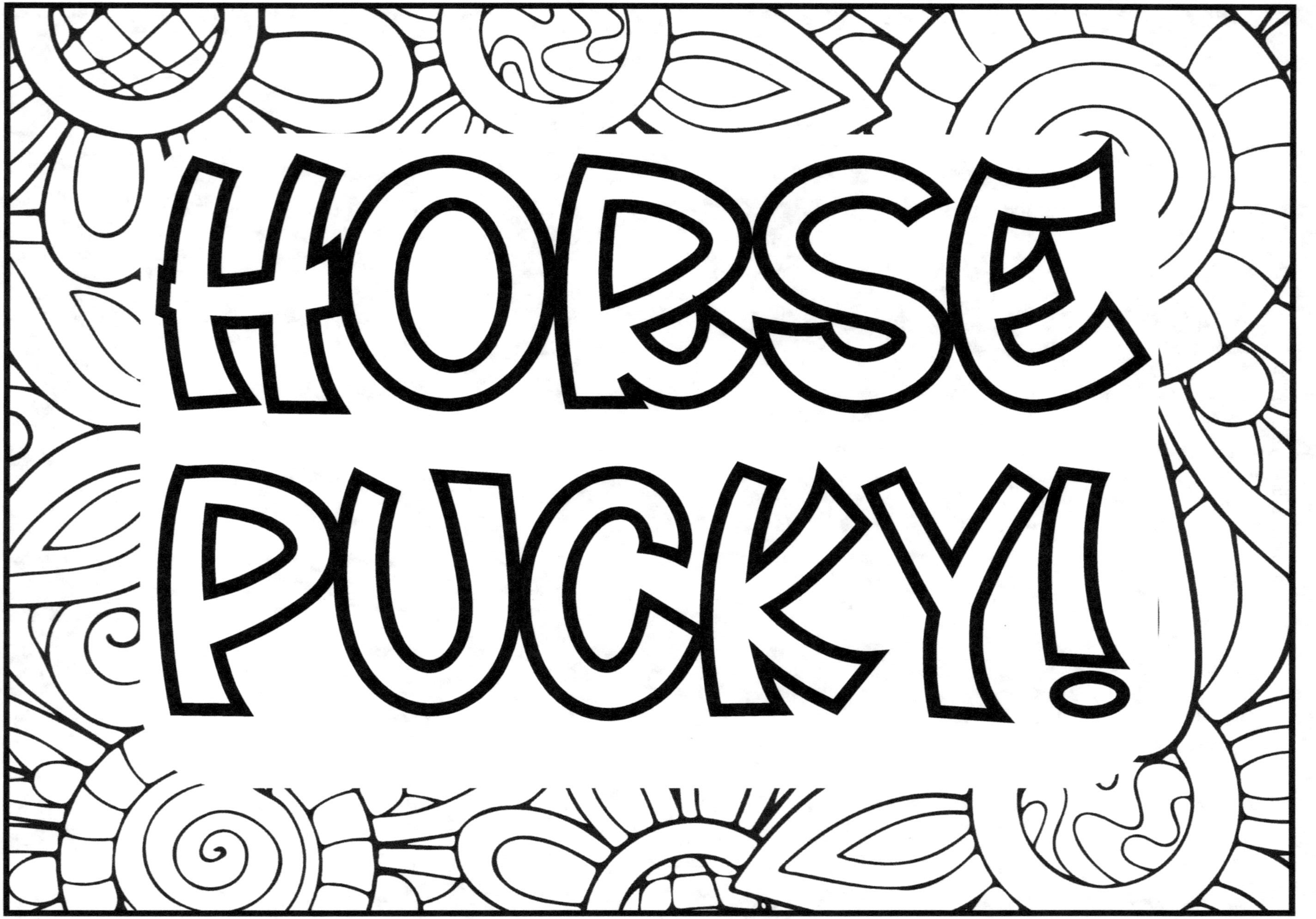
HORSE
PUCKY!

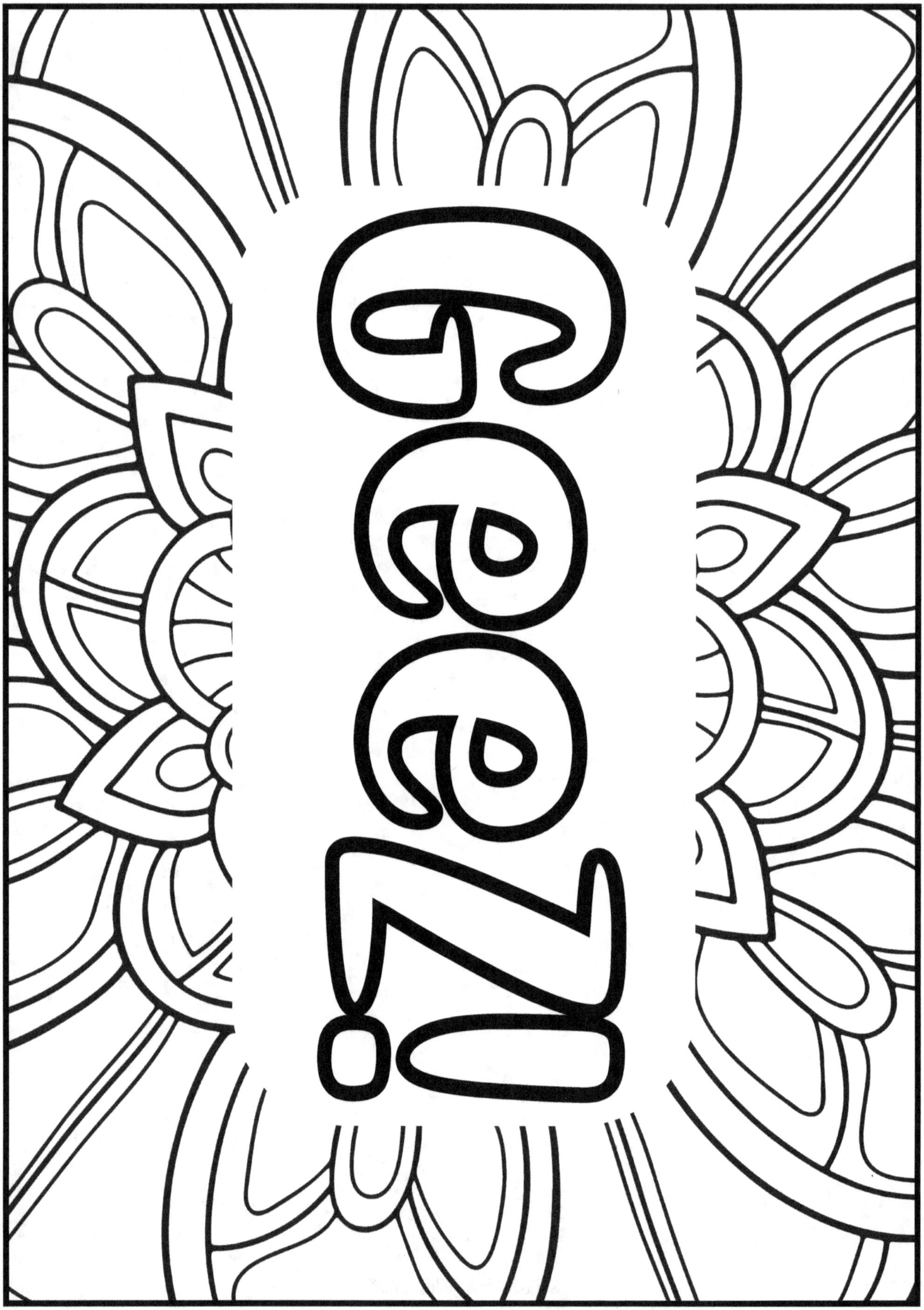
Geez!

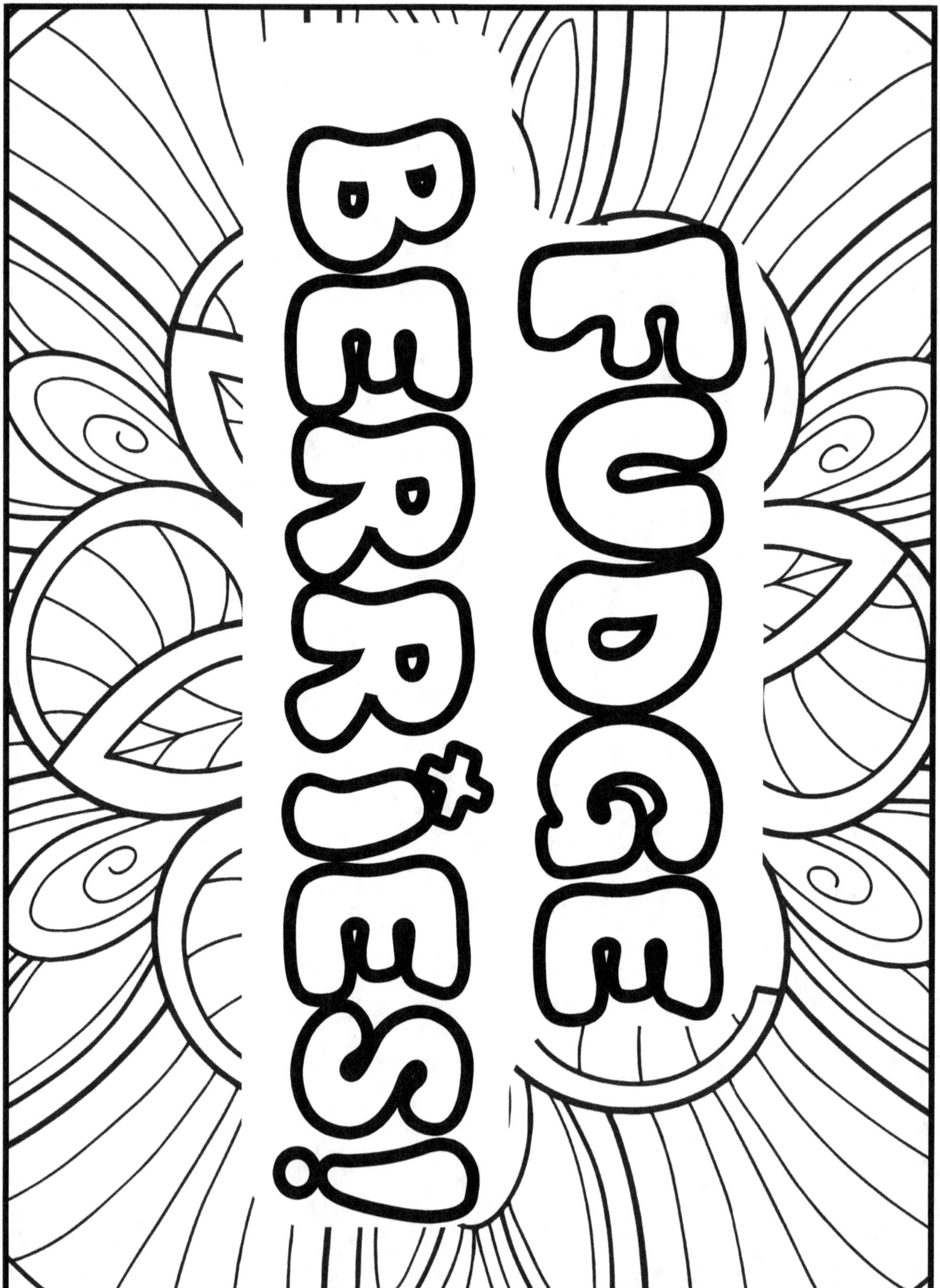
FUDGE
BERRIES!

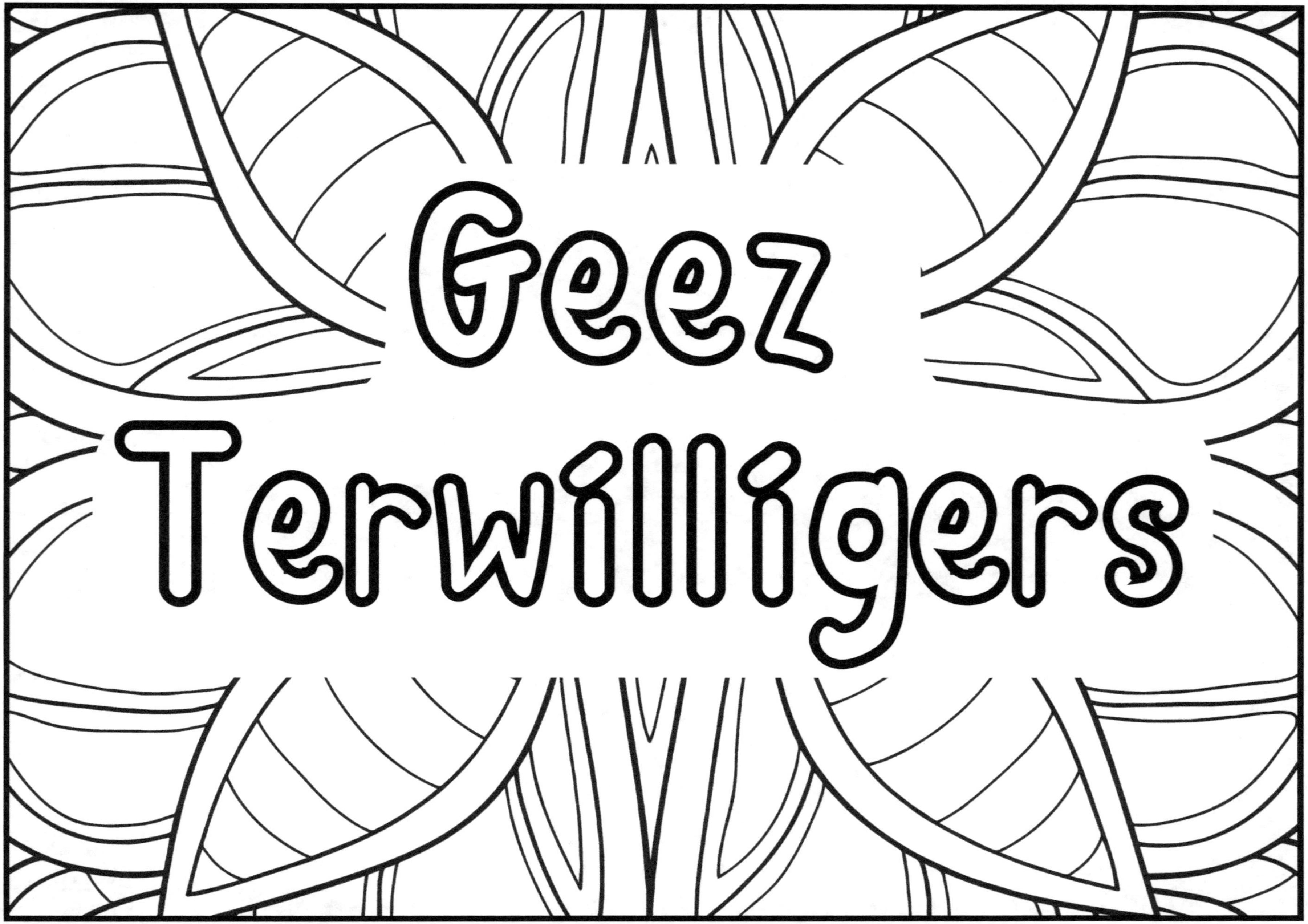
Geez
Terwilligers

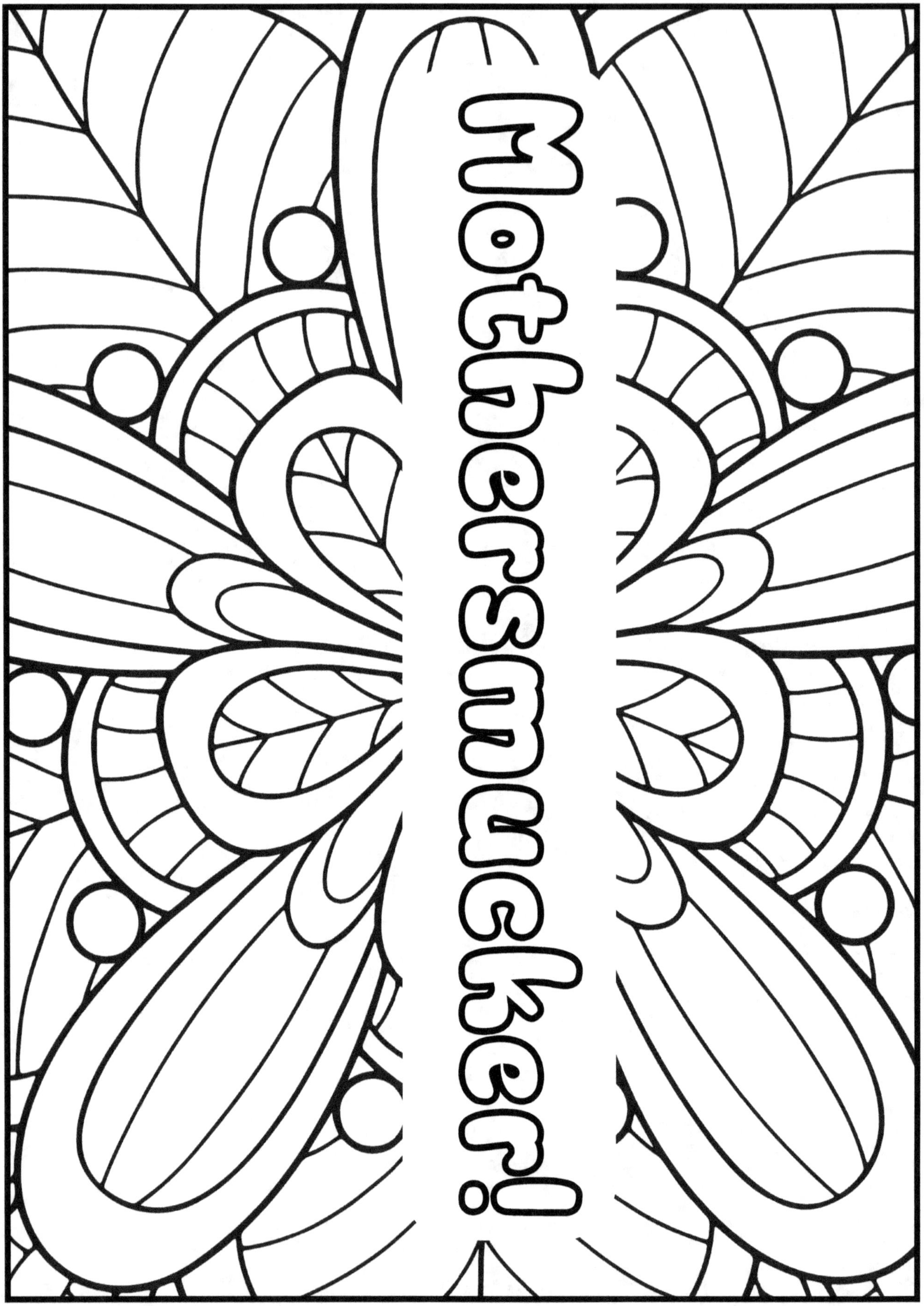
Mothersmucker!

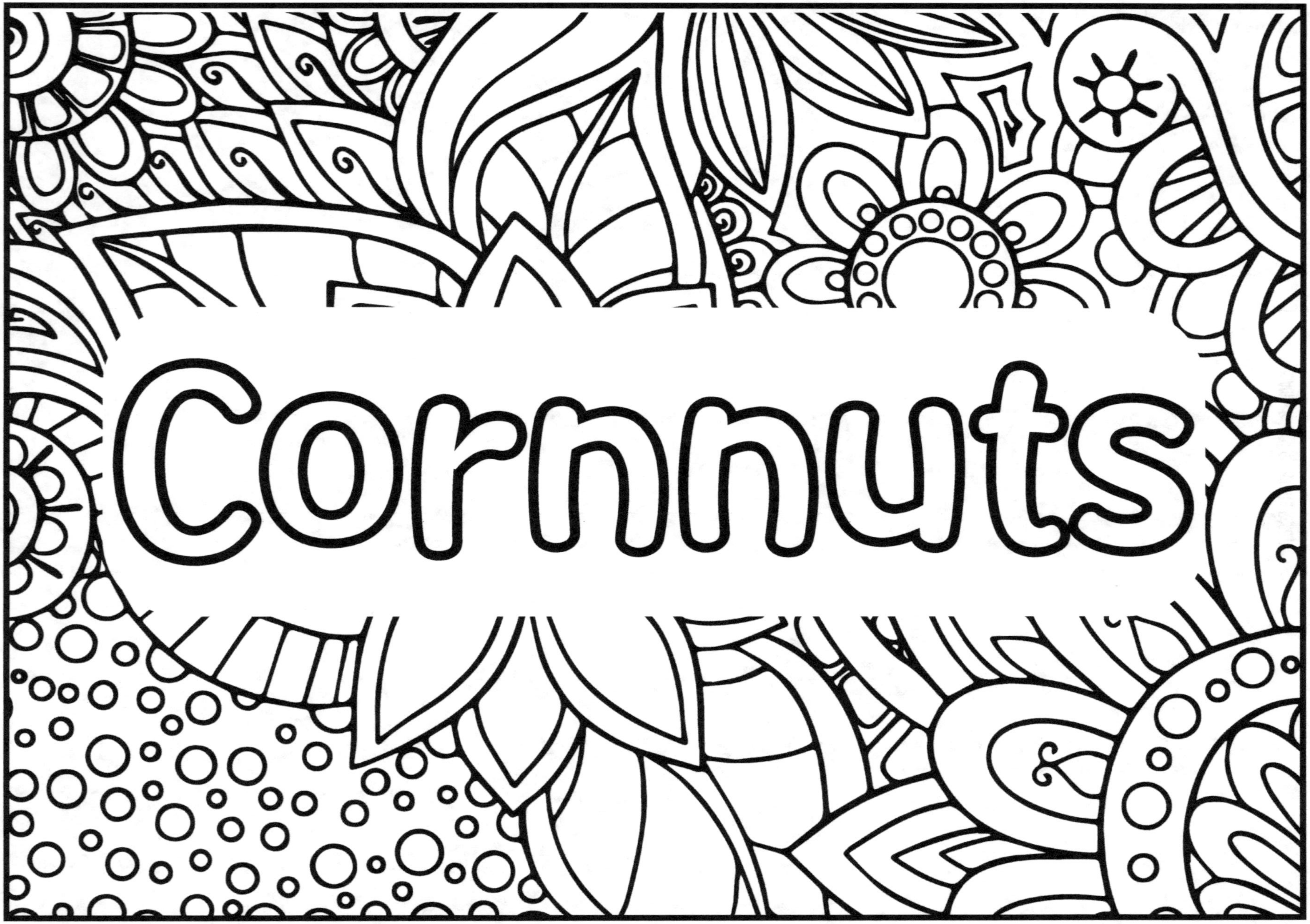
Cornnuts

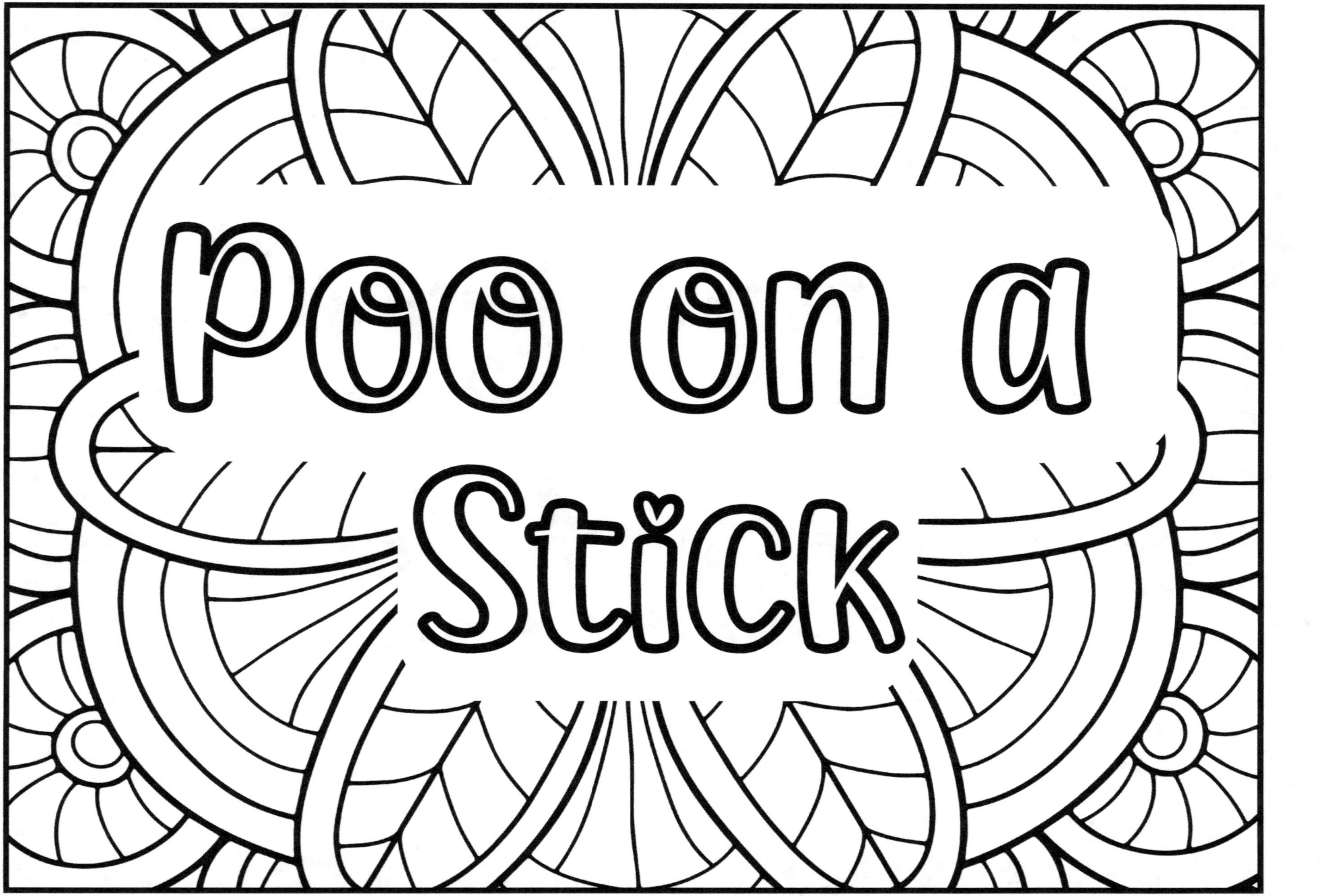
Poo on a
Stick

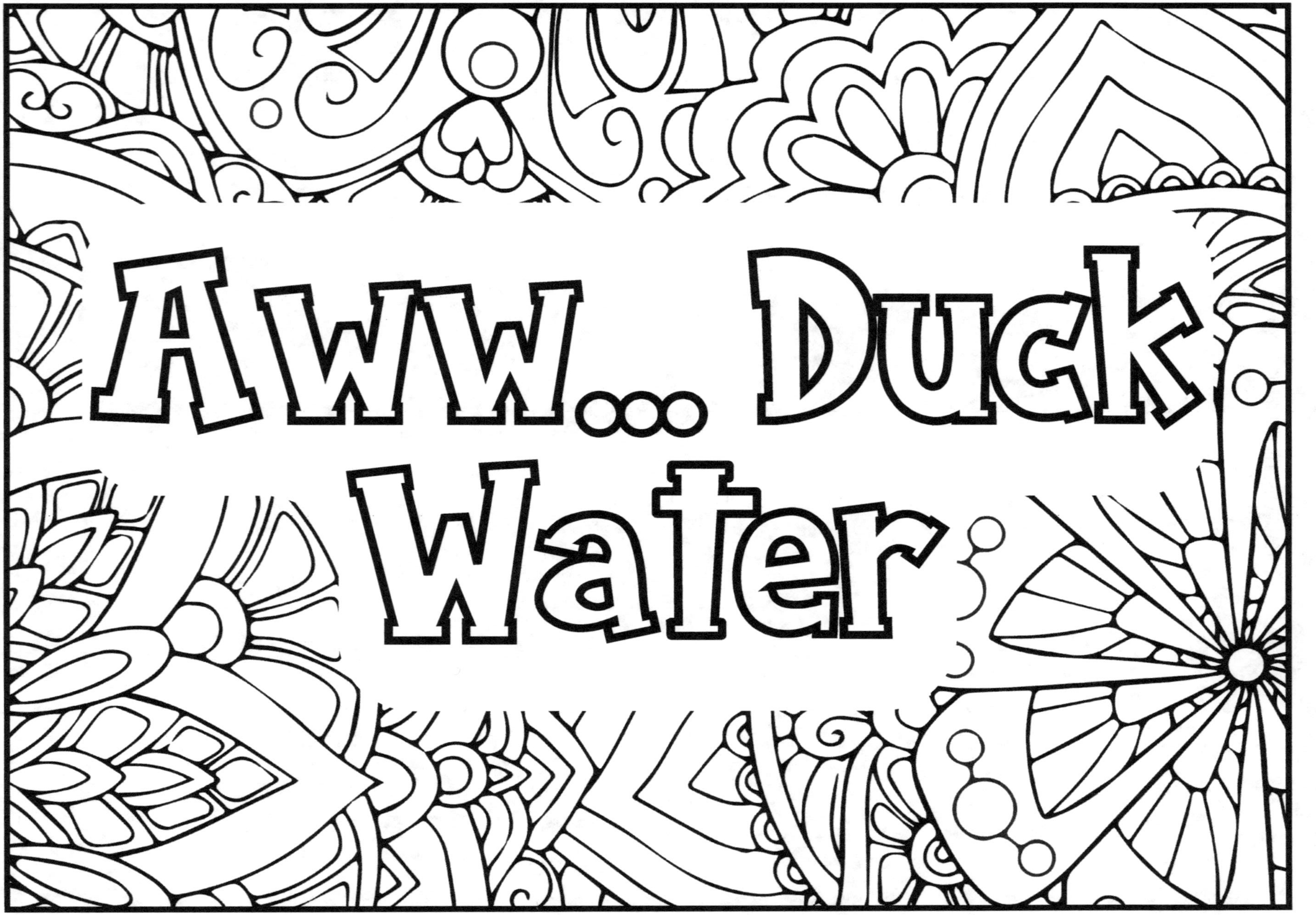
Aww... Duck
Water

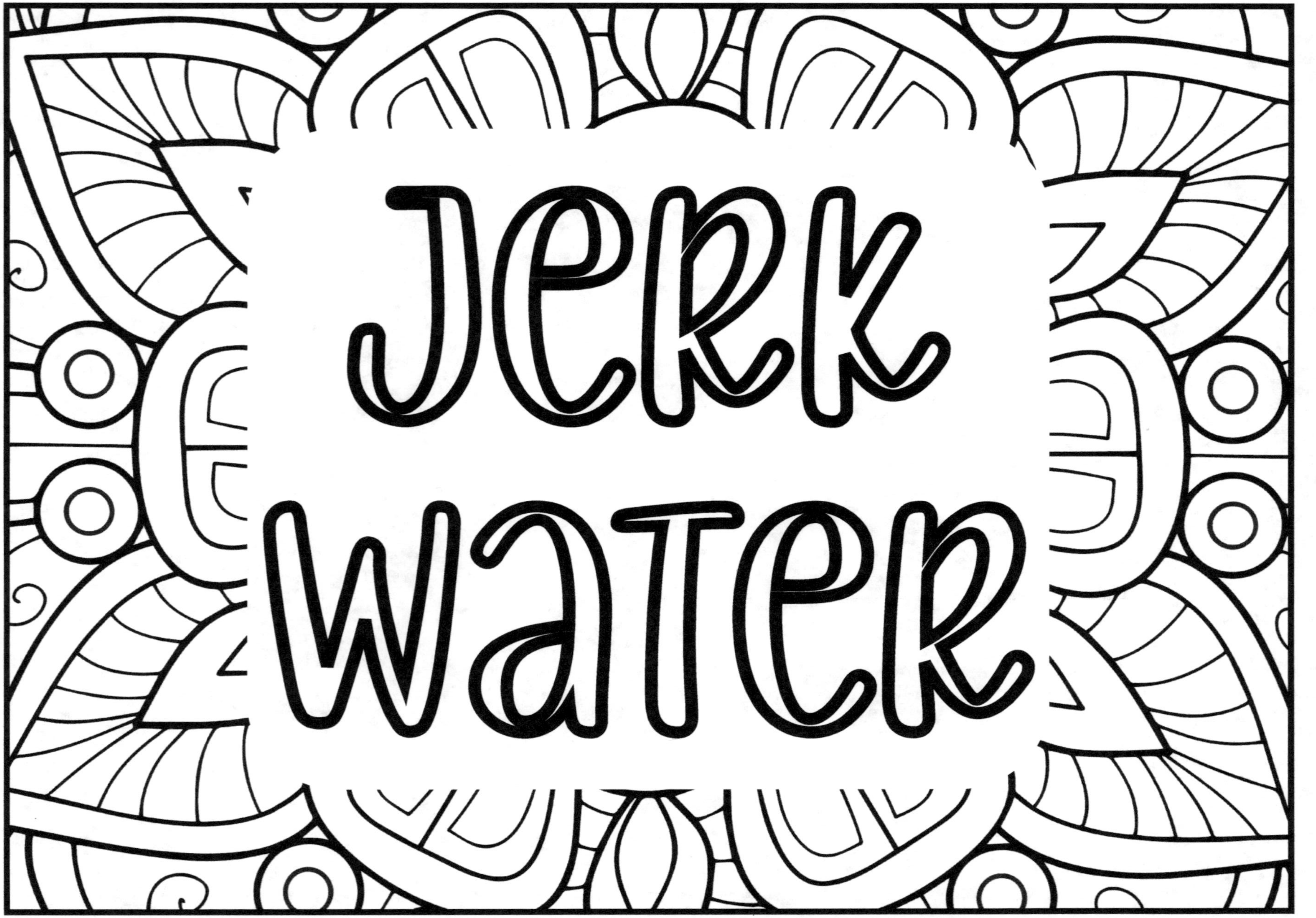
Jerk
Water

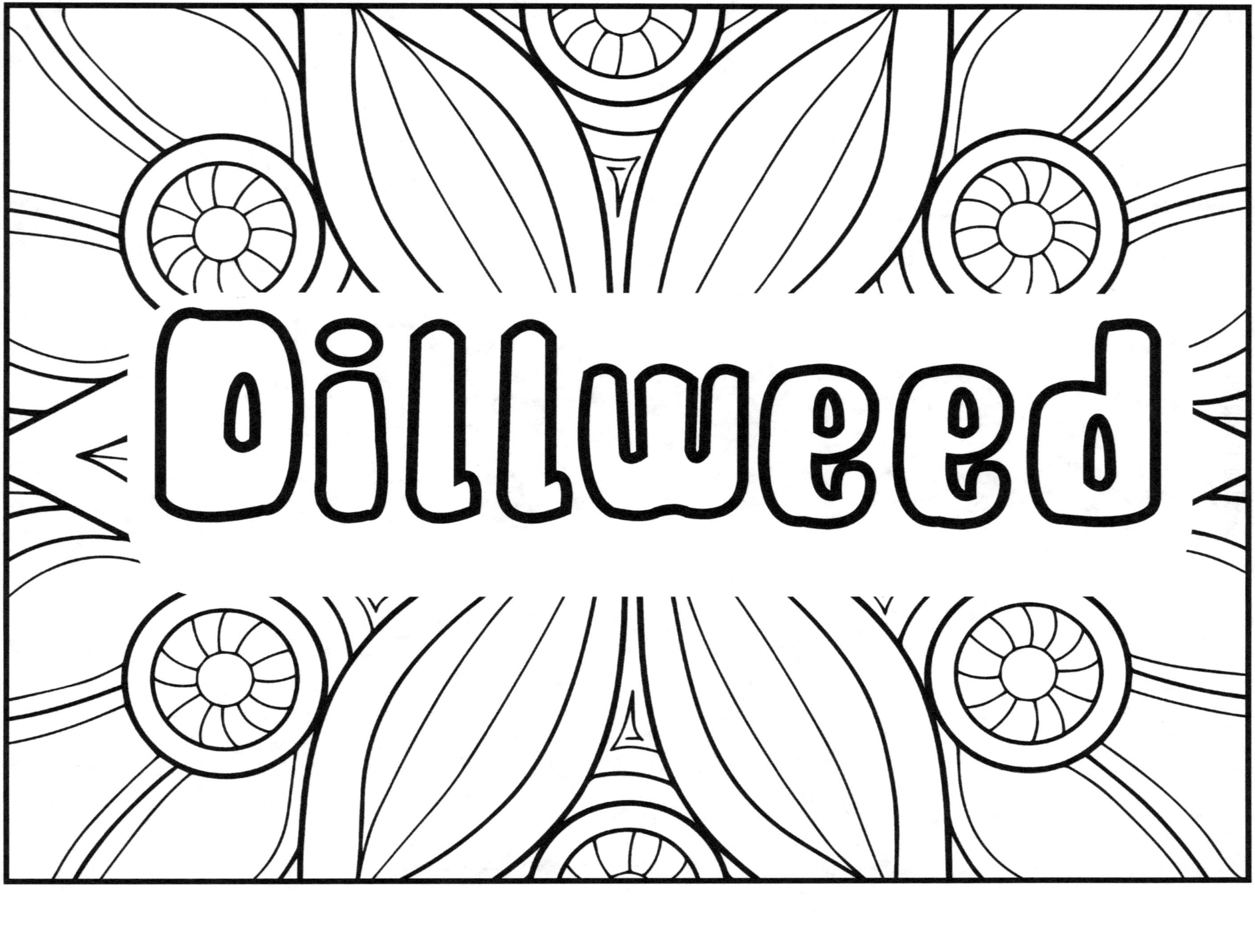
Dillweed

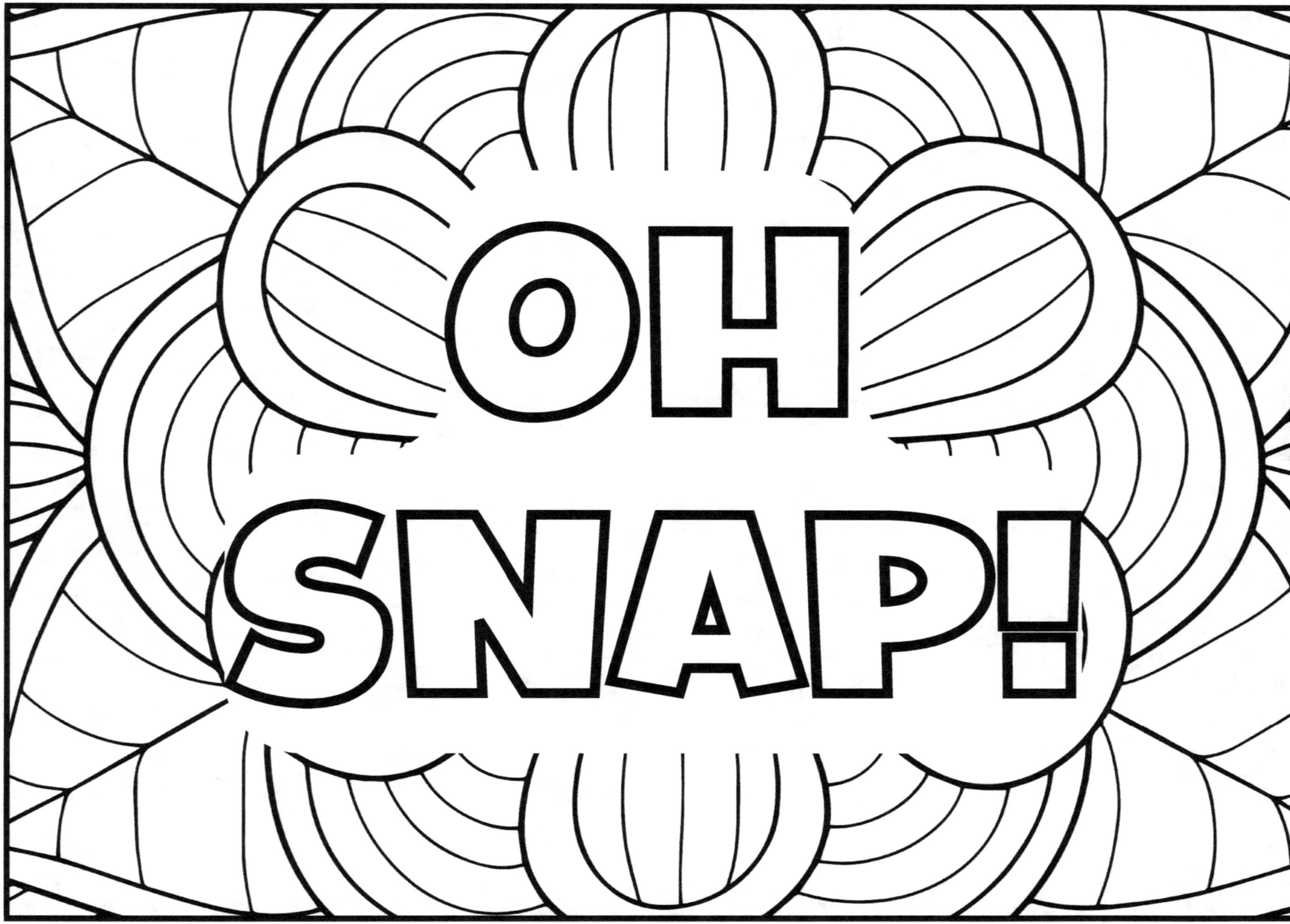
OH
SNAP!

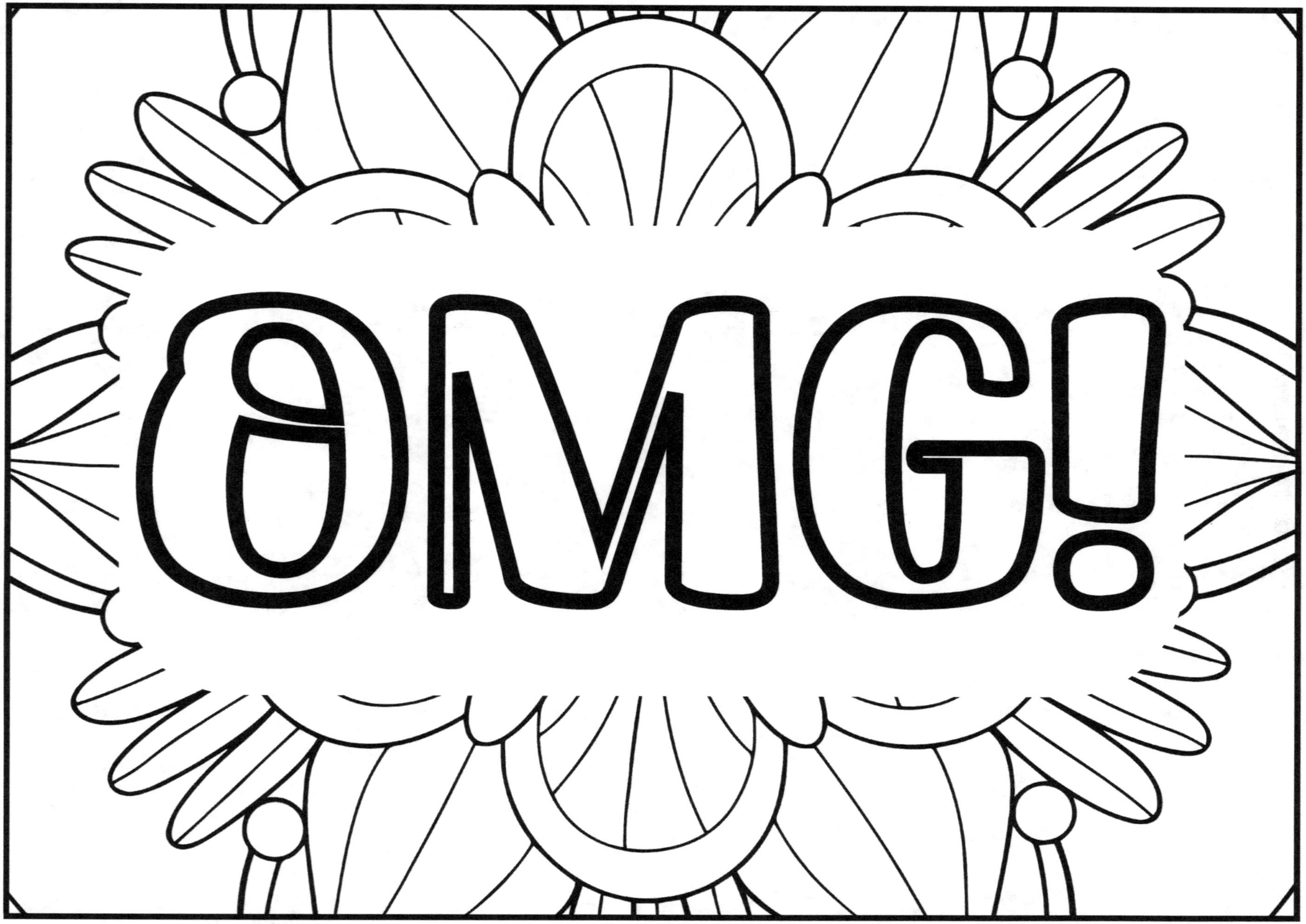
OMG!

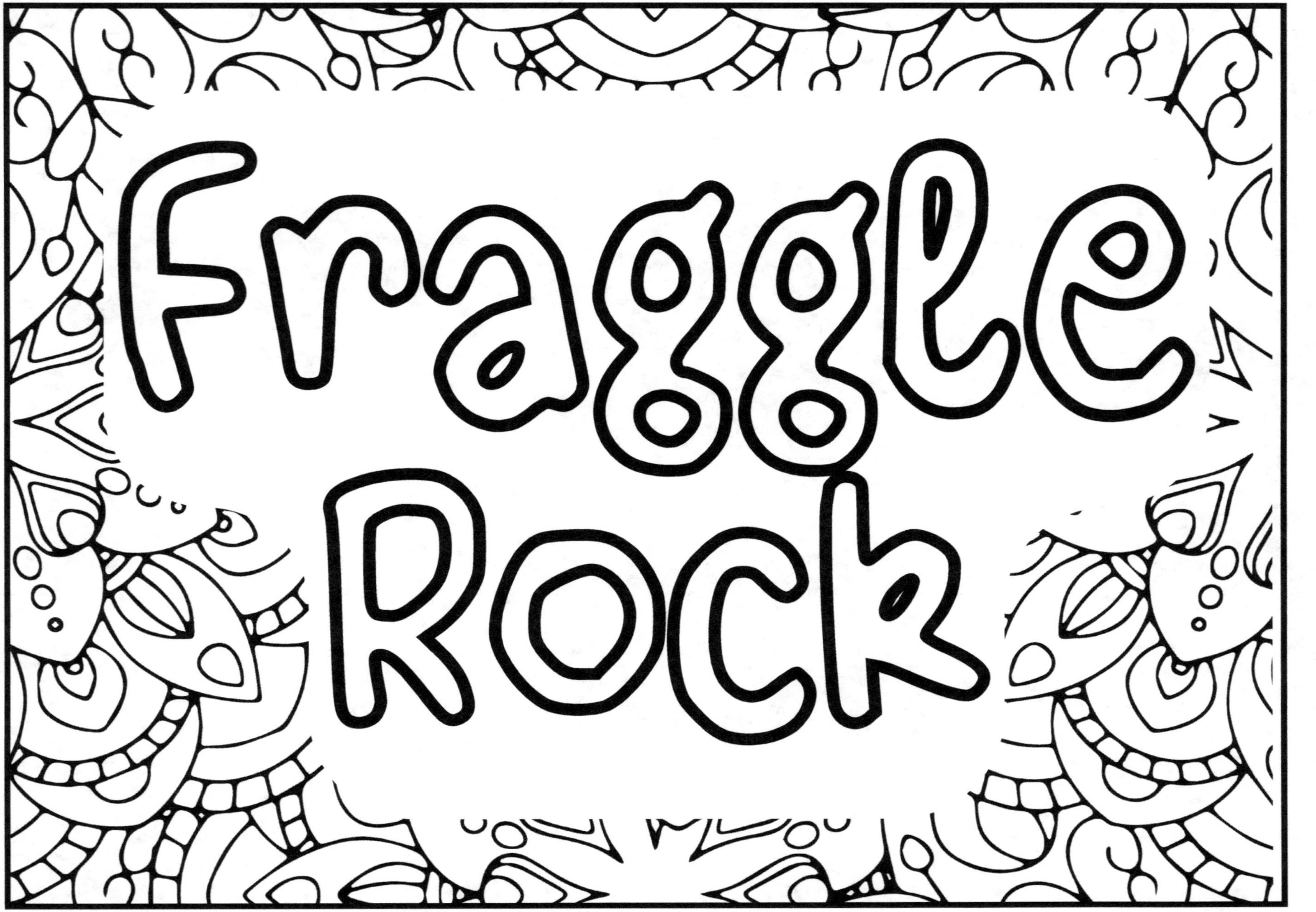
Fraggle Rock

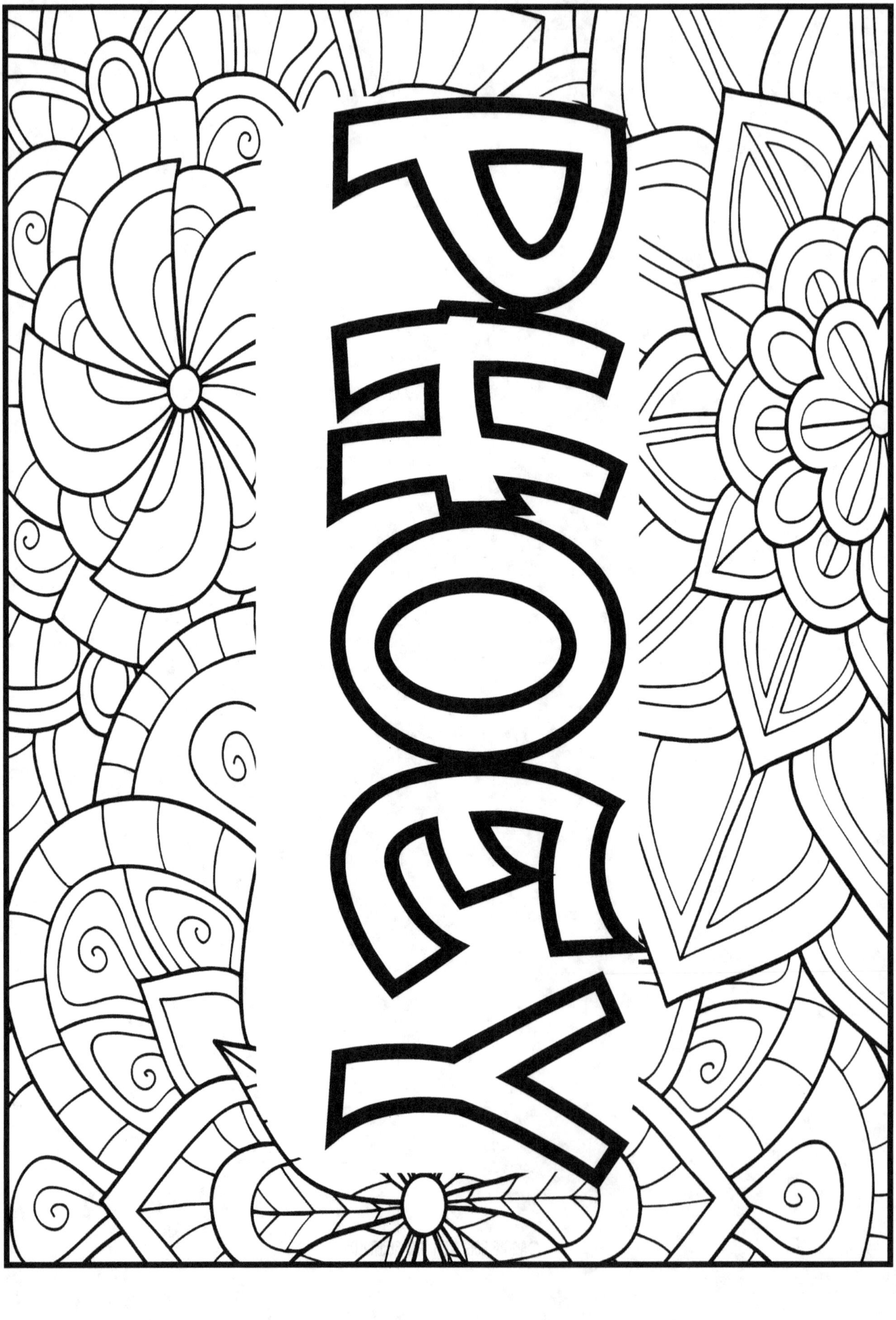
PHOOEY

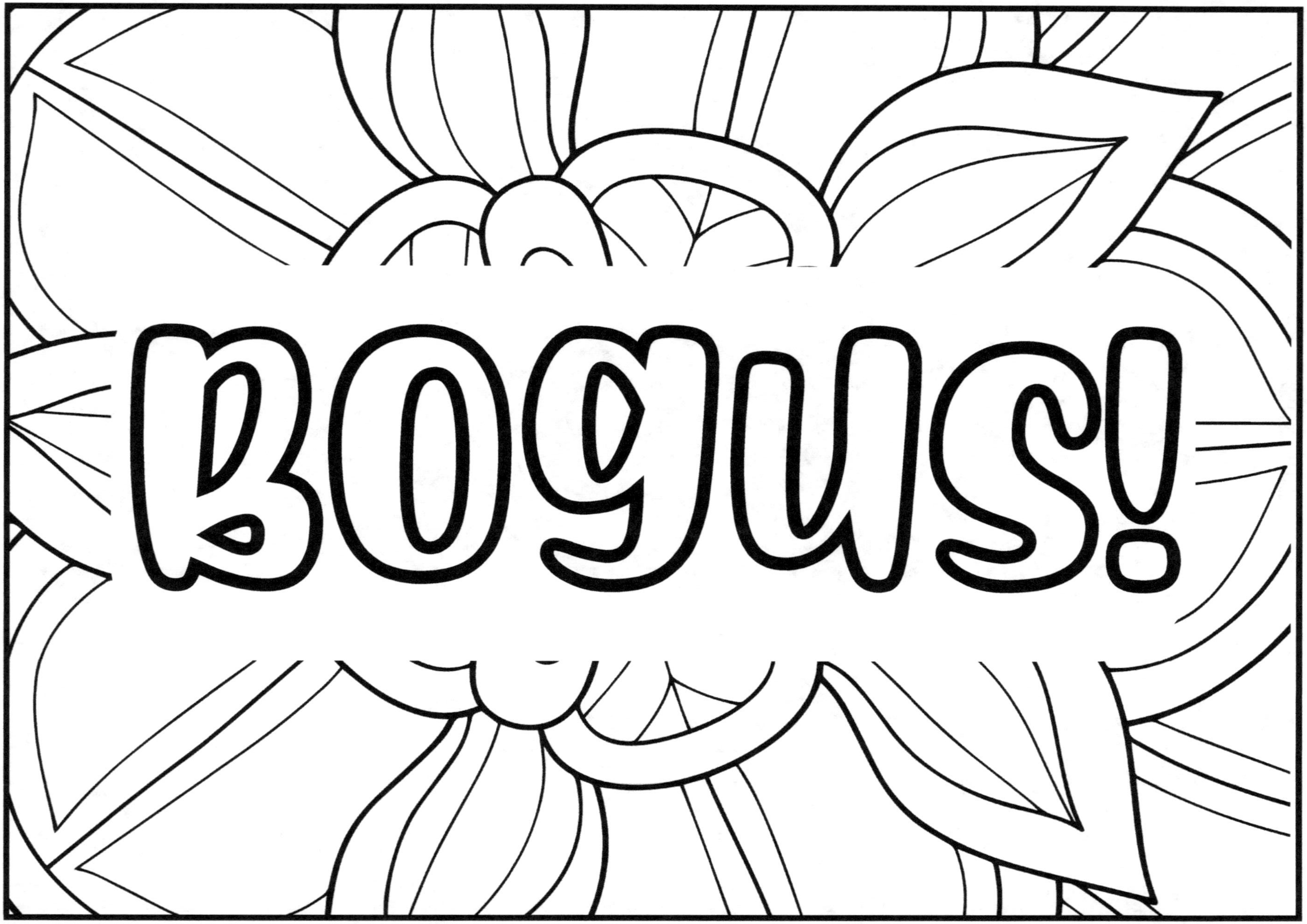
BOGUS!

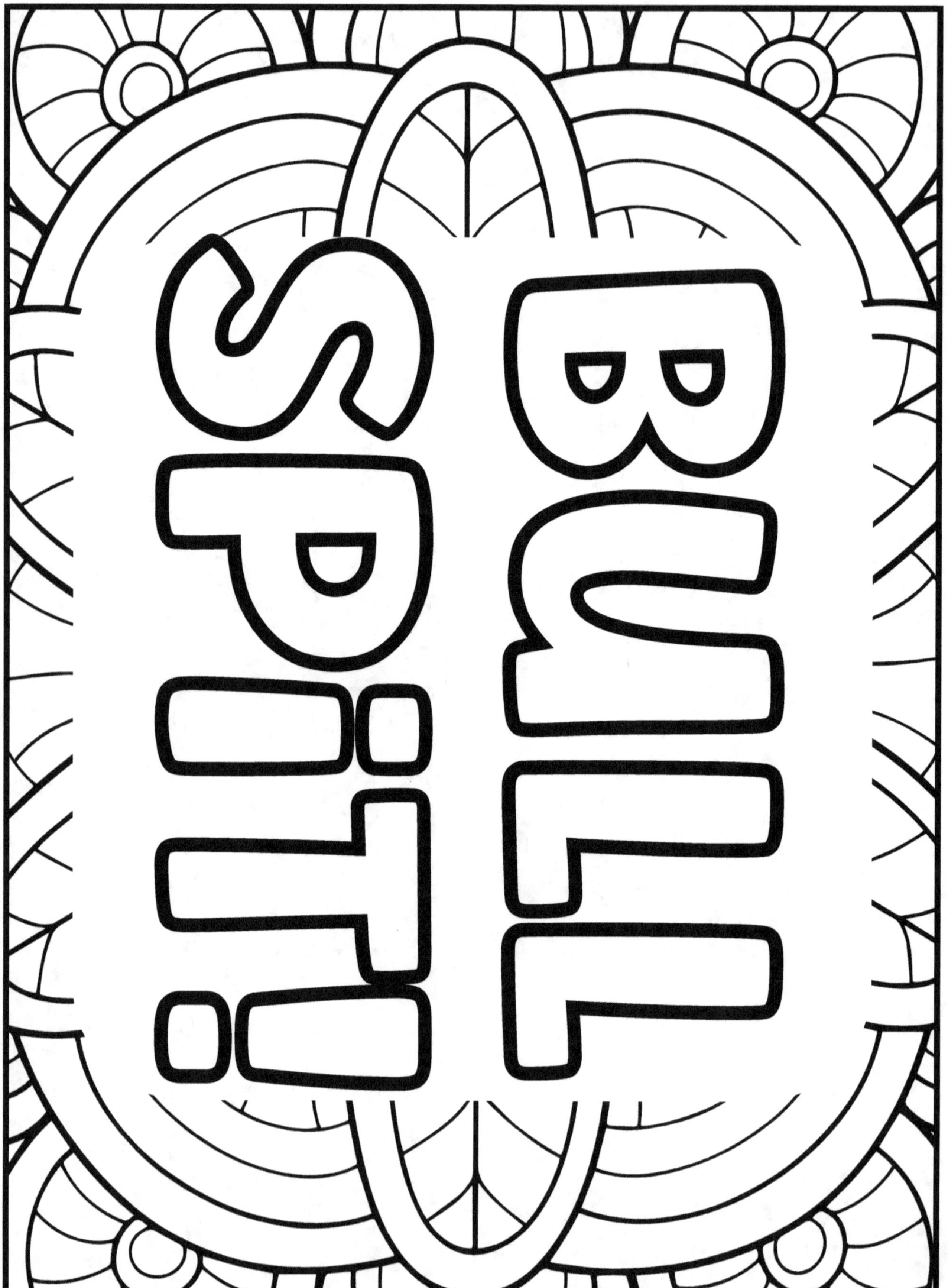

BULL
SPIT!

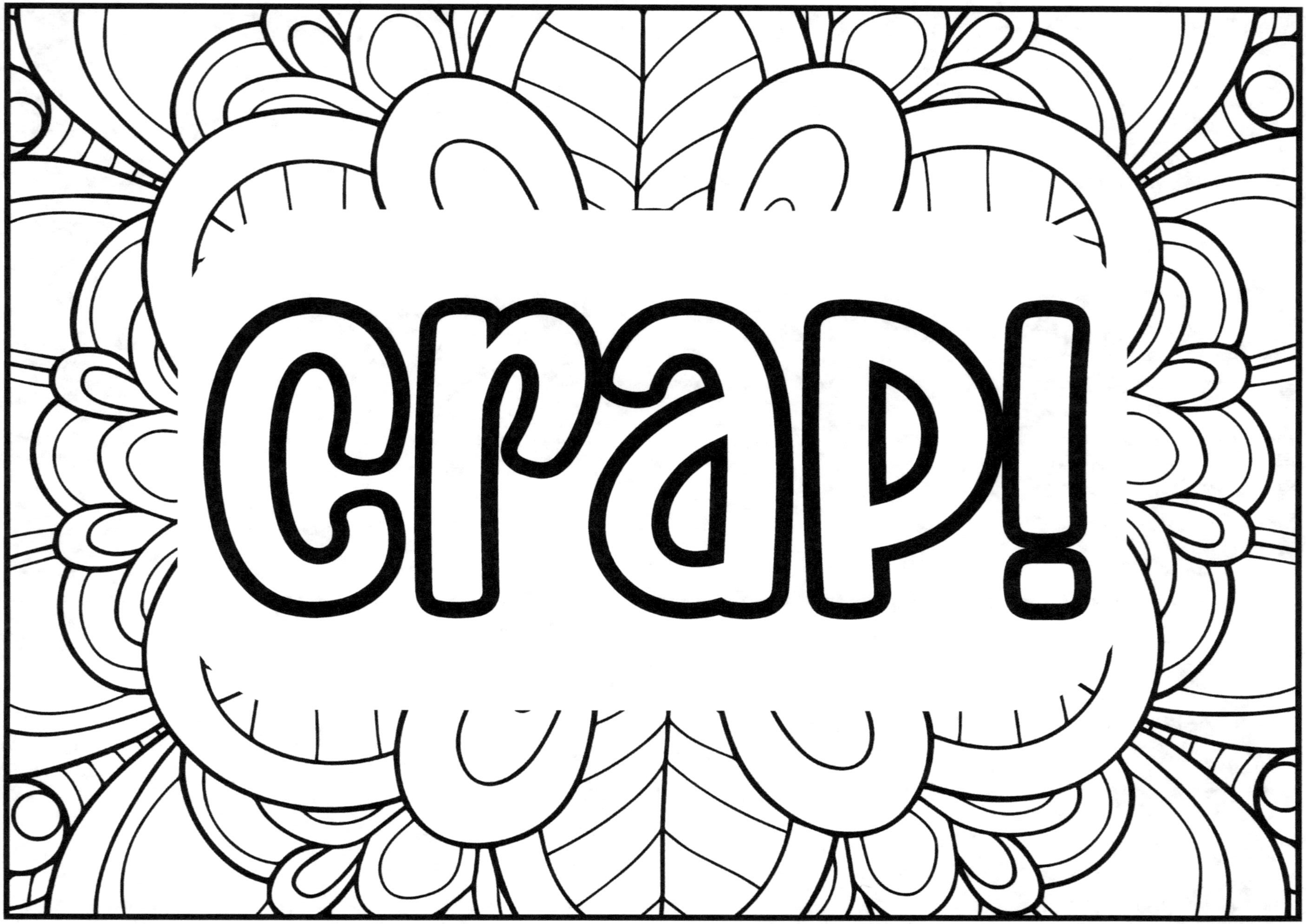
crap!

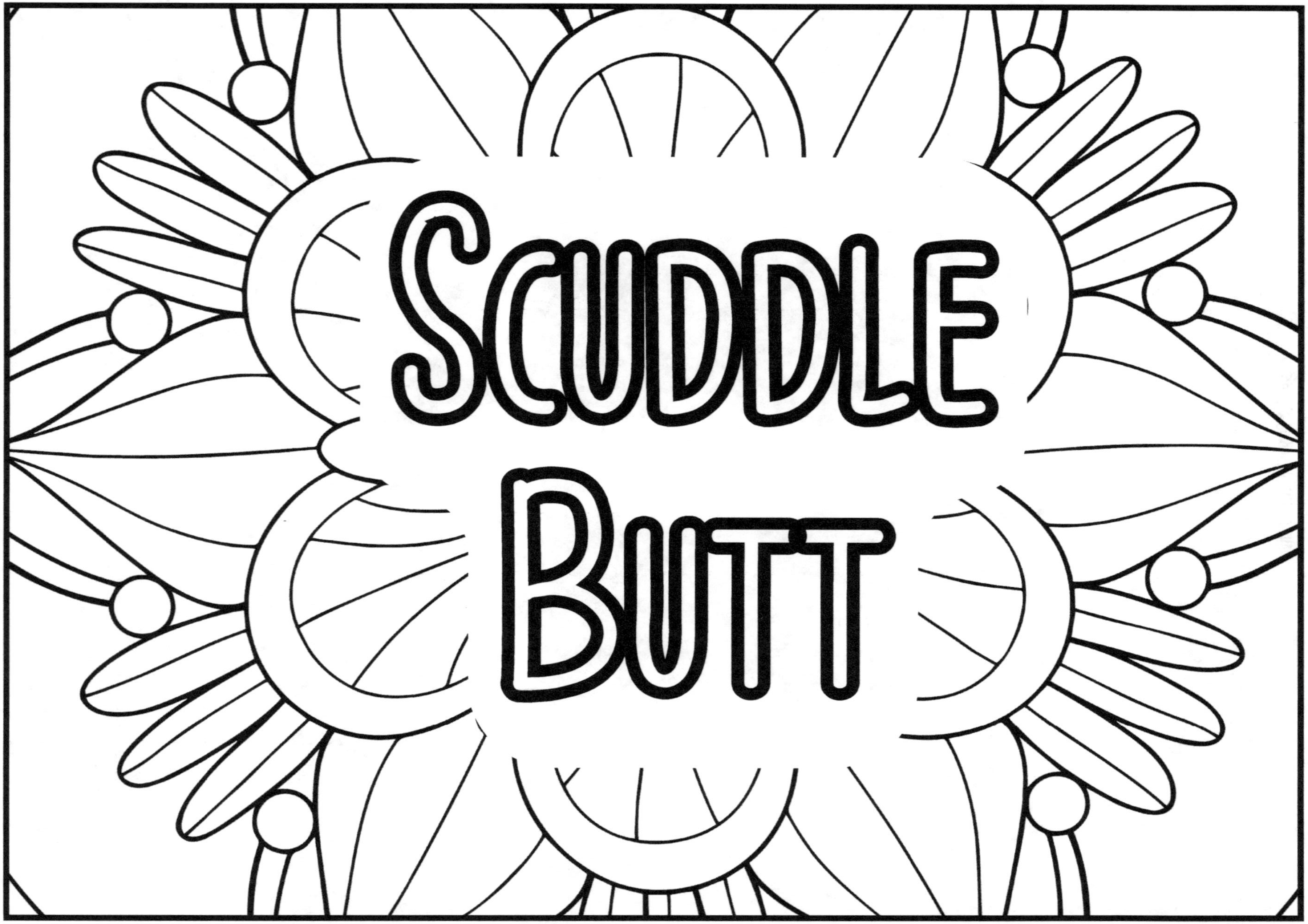
SCUDDLE
BUTT

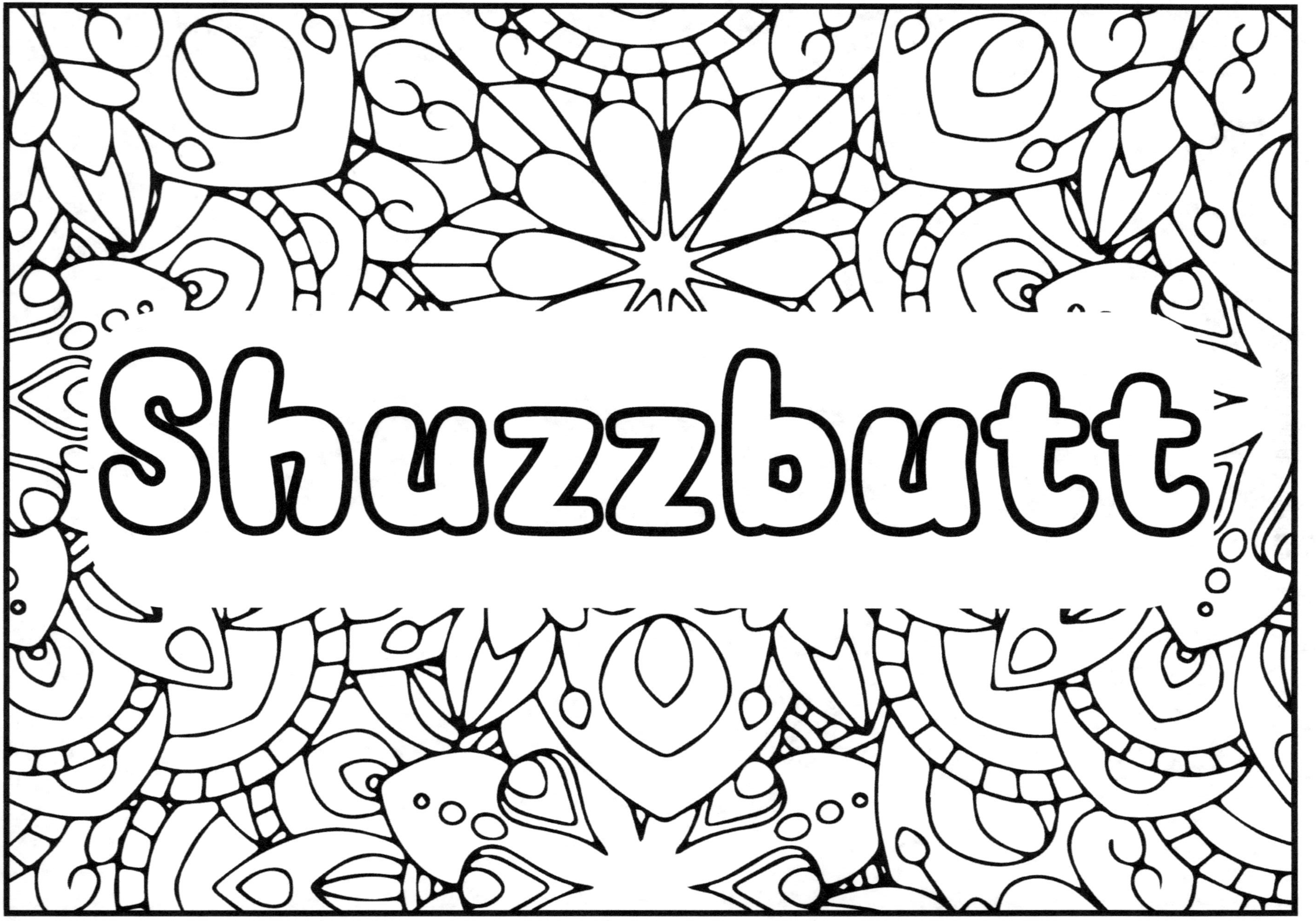
Shuzzbutt

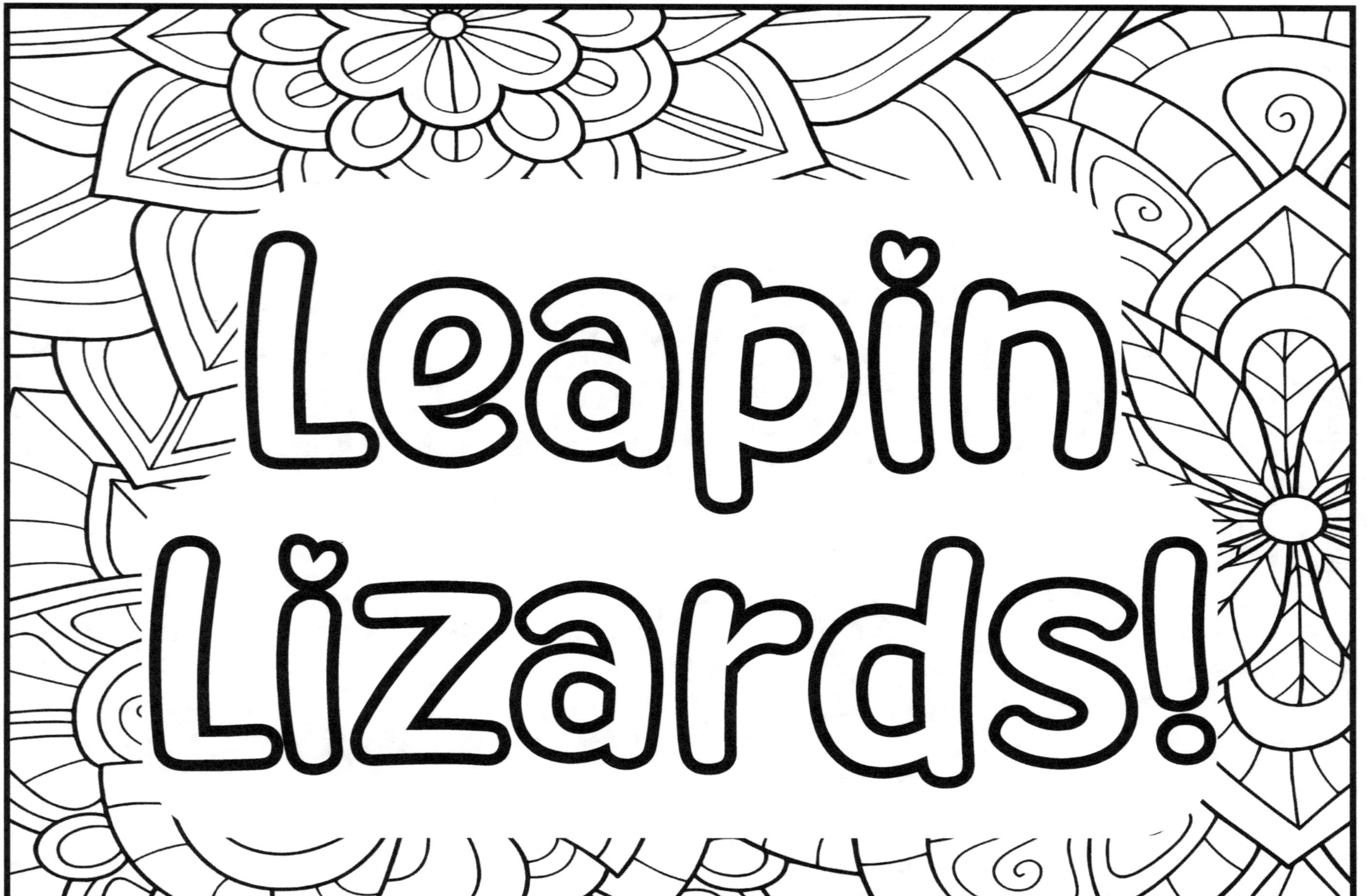
Leapin
Lizards!

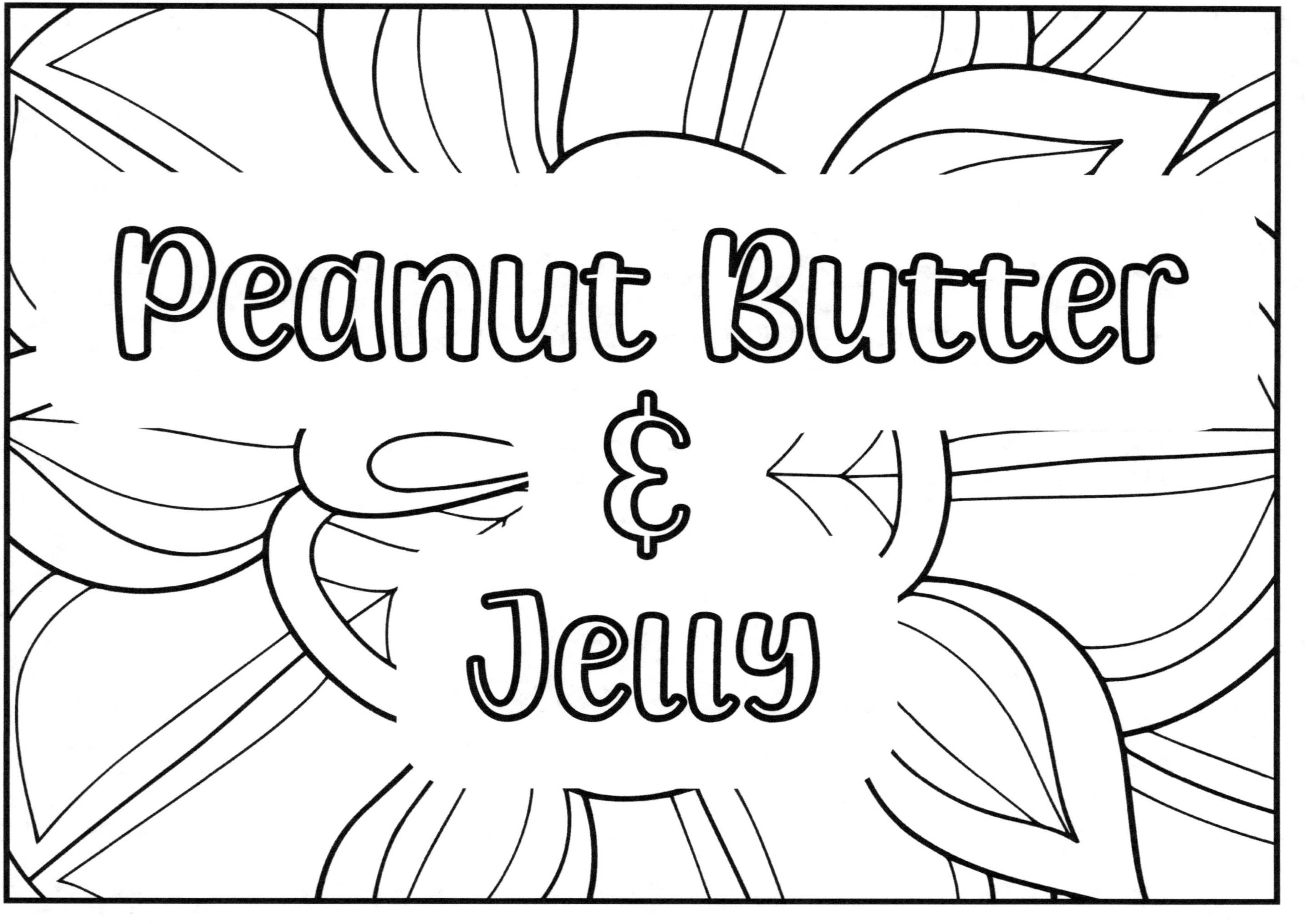
Peanut Butter
&
Jelly

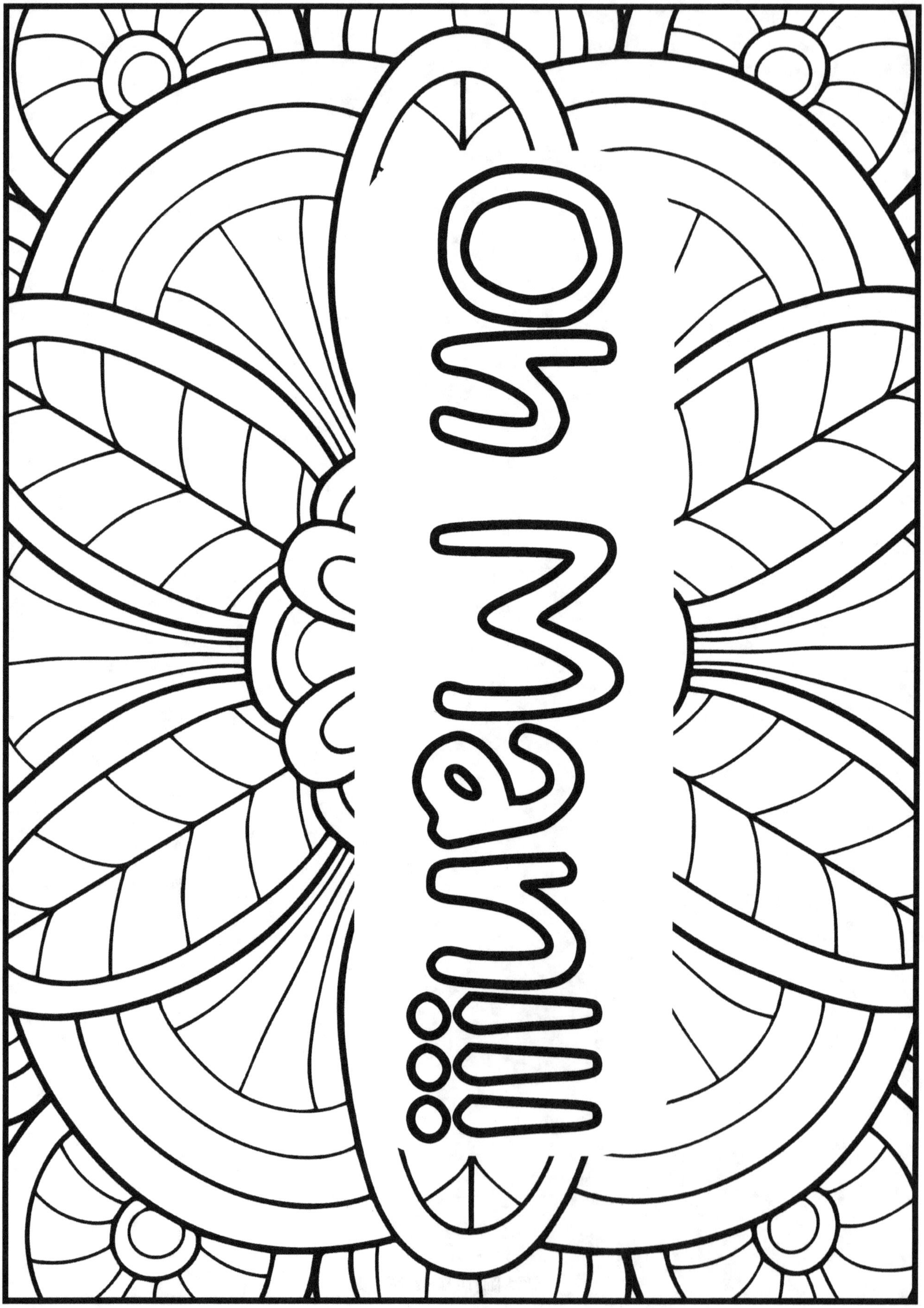
Oh Man!!!

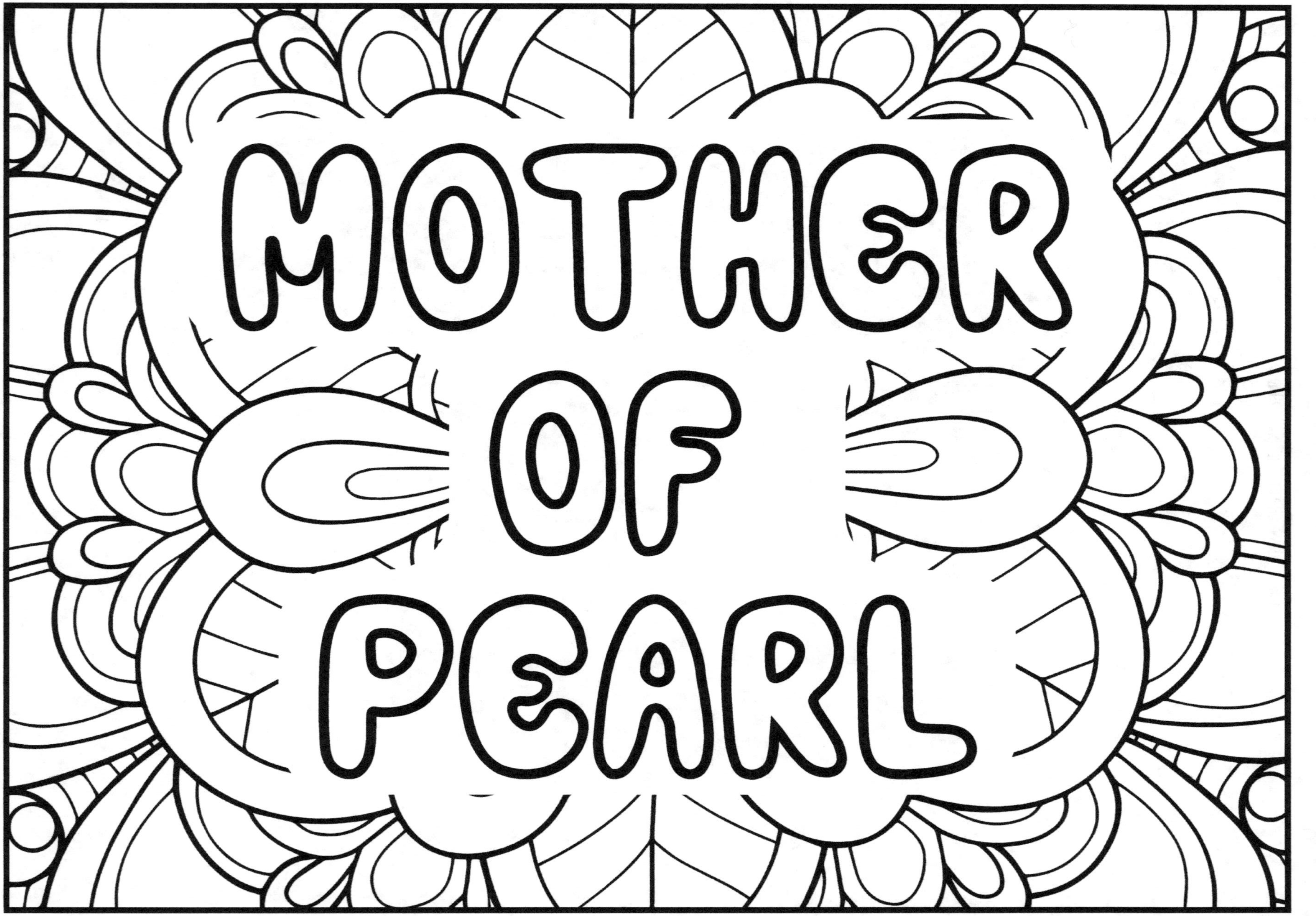
MOTHER
OF
PEARL

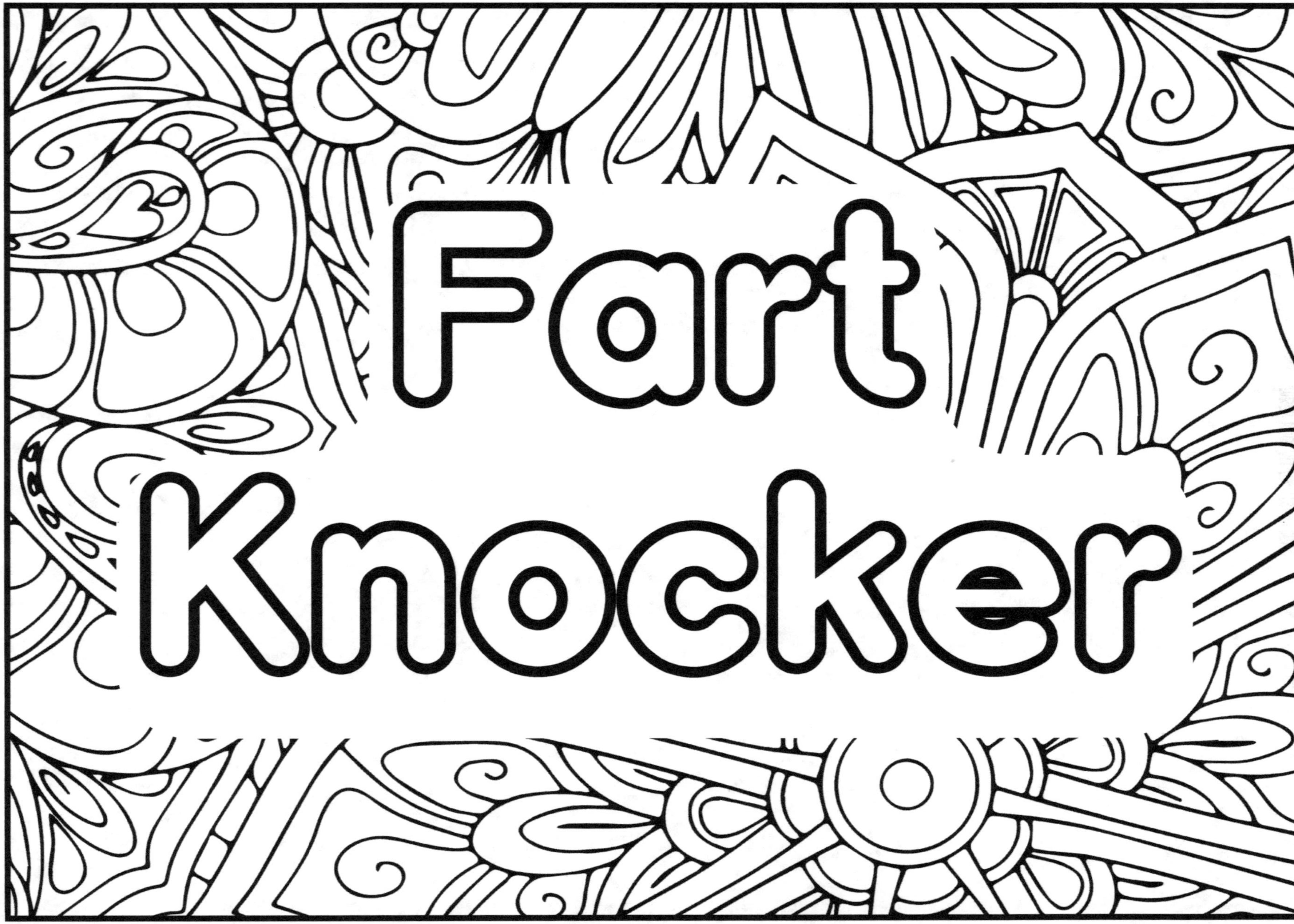
Fart
Knocker

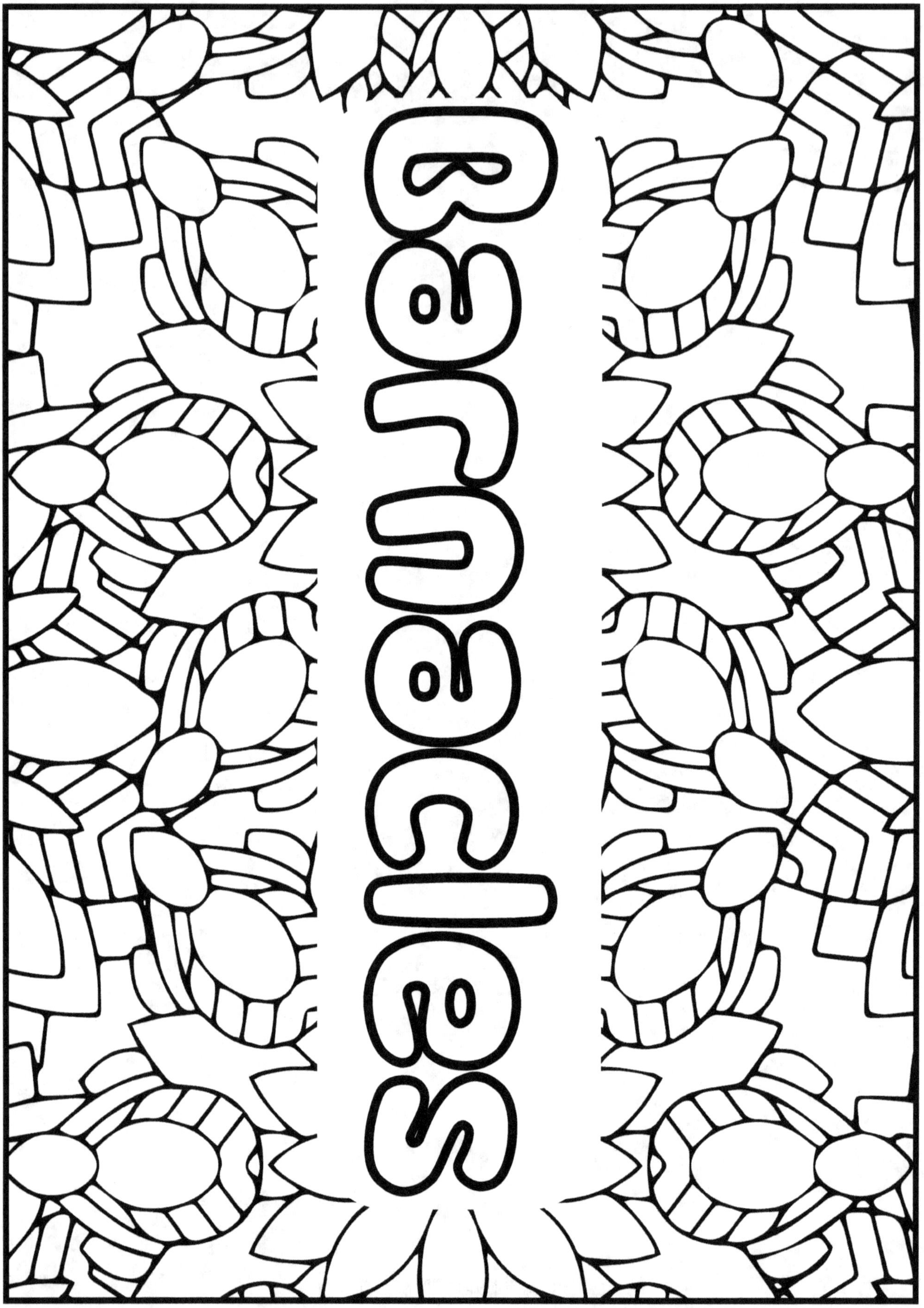
Barnacles

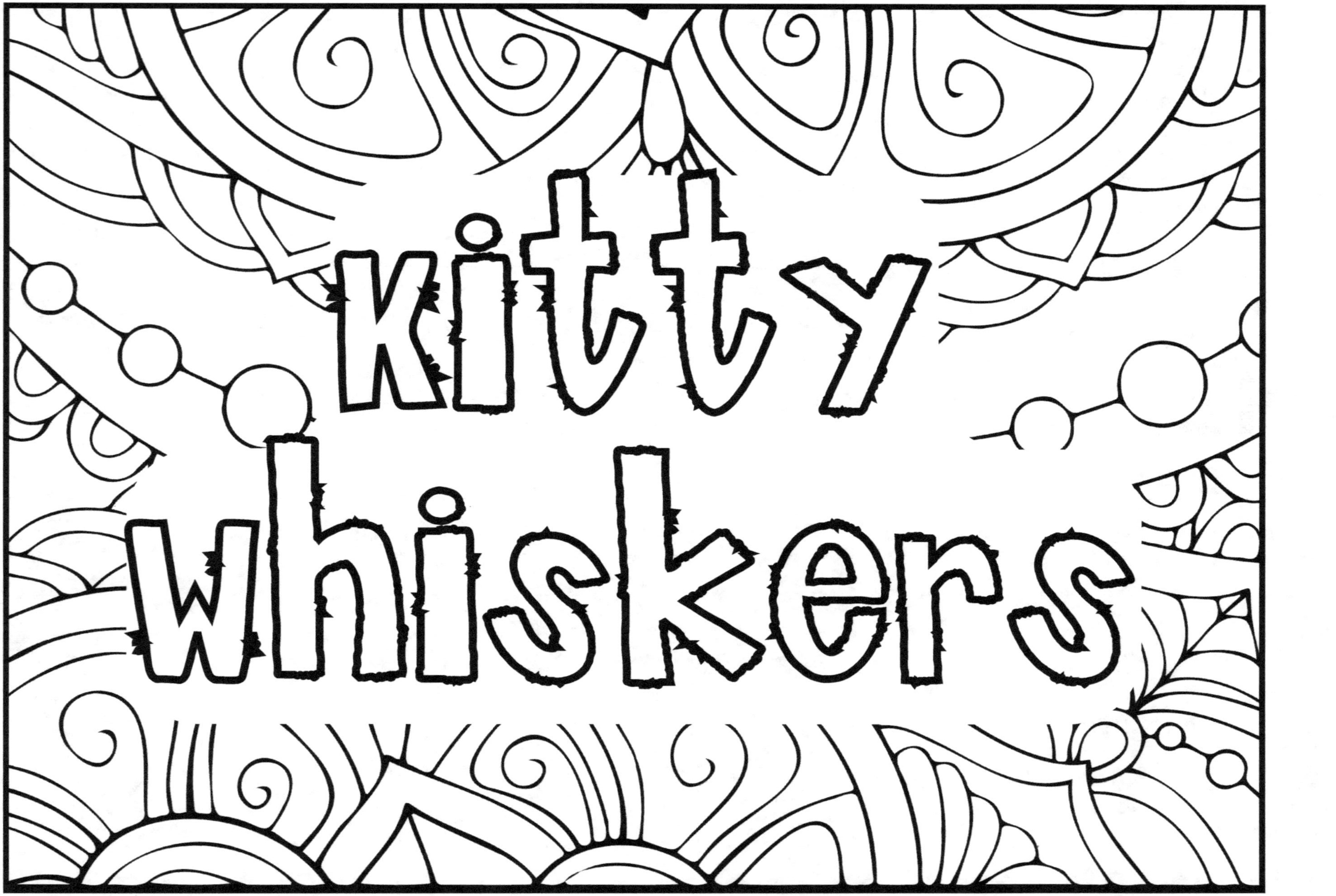
kitty
whiskers

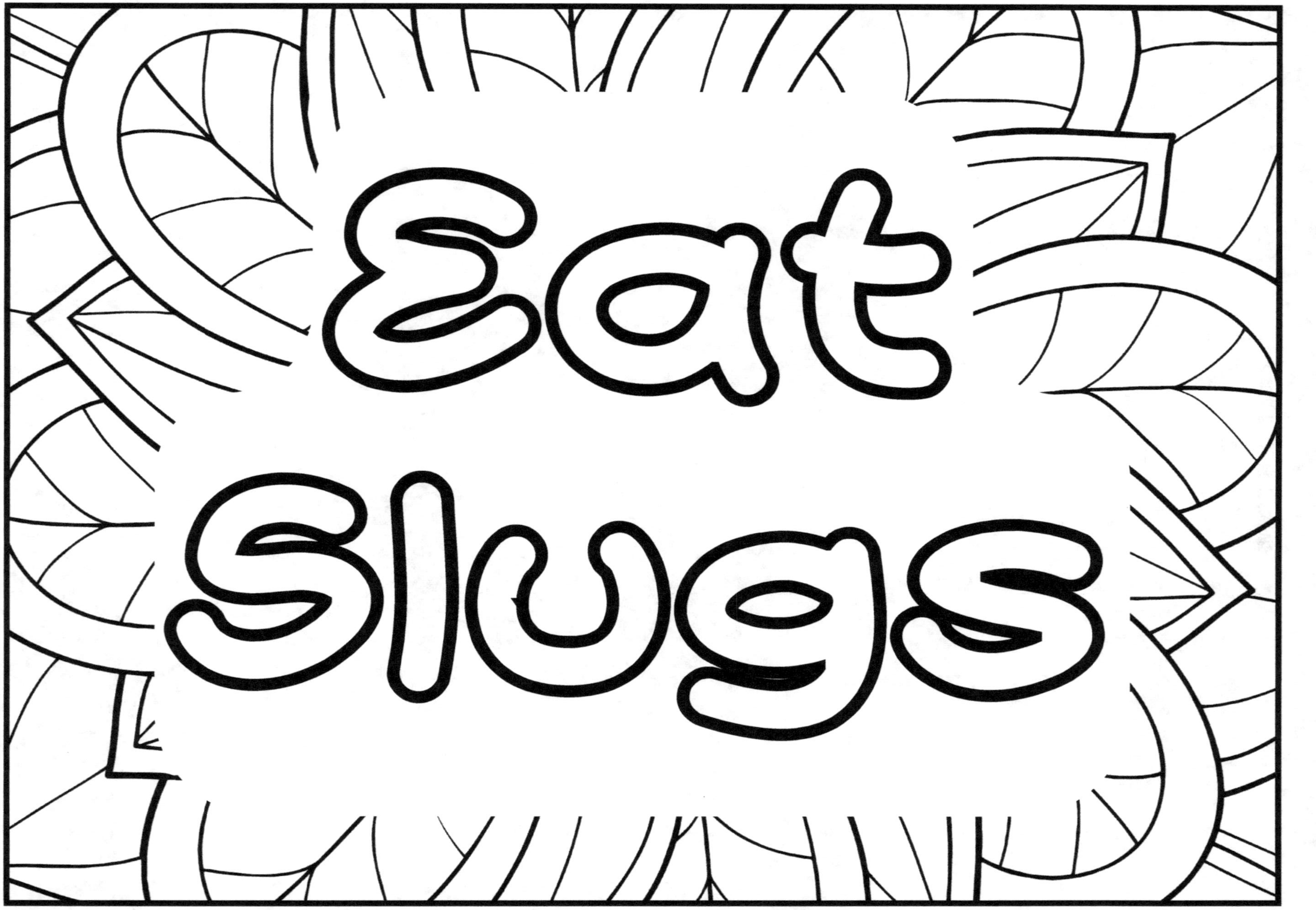
Eat
Slugs

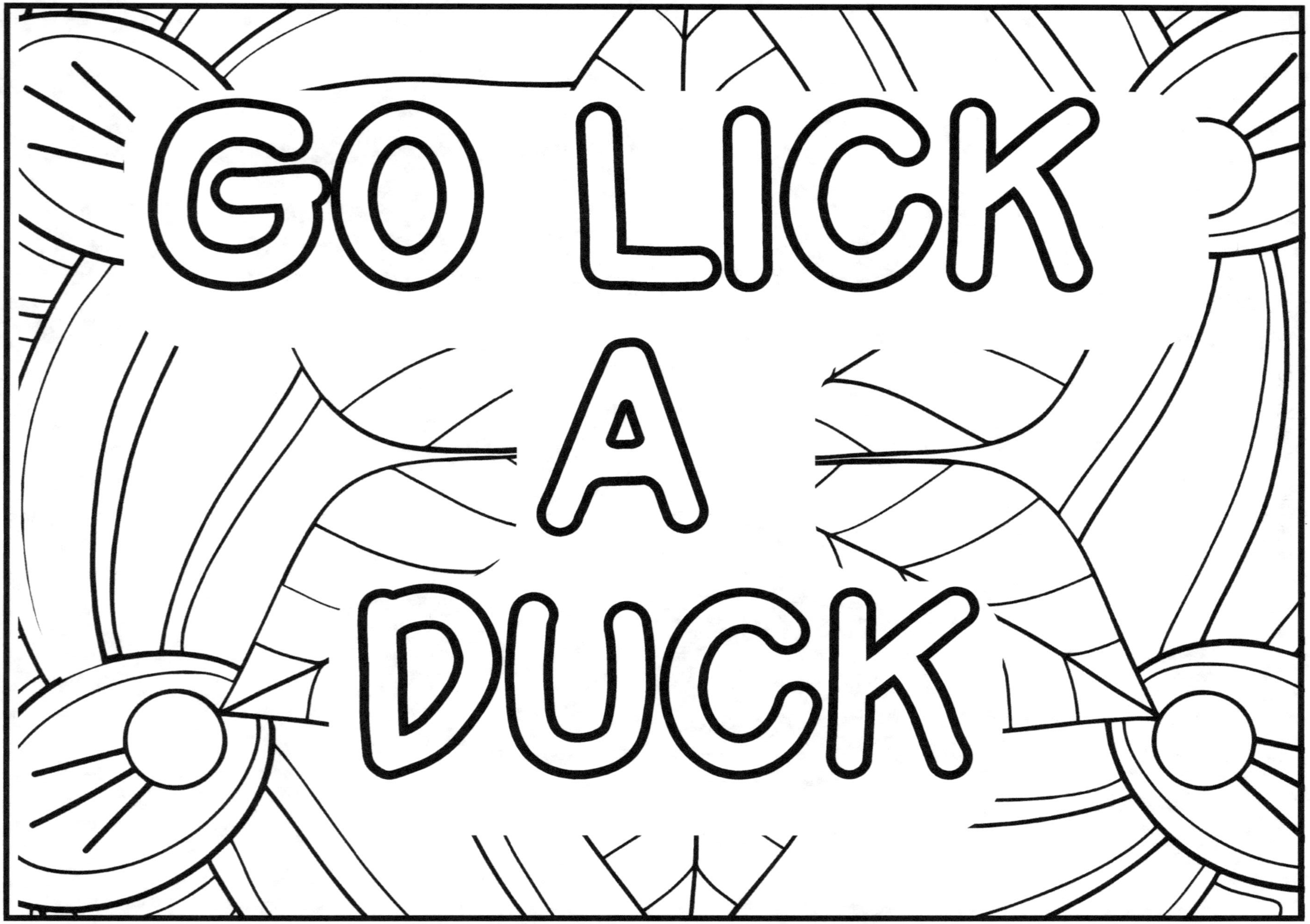
GO LICK
A
DUCK

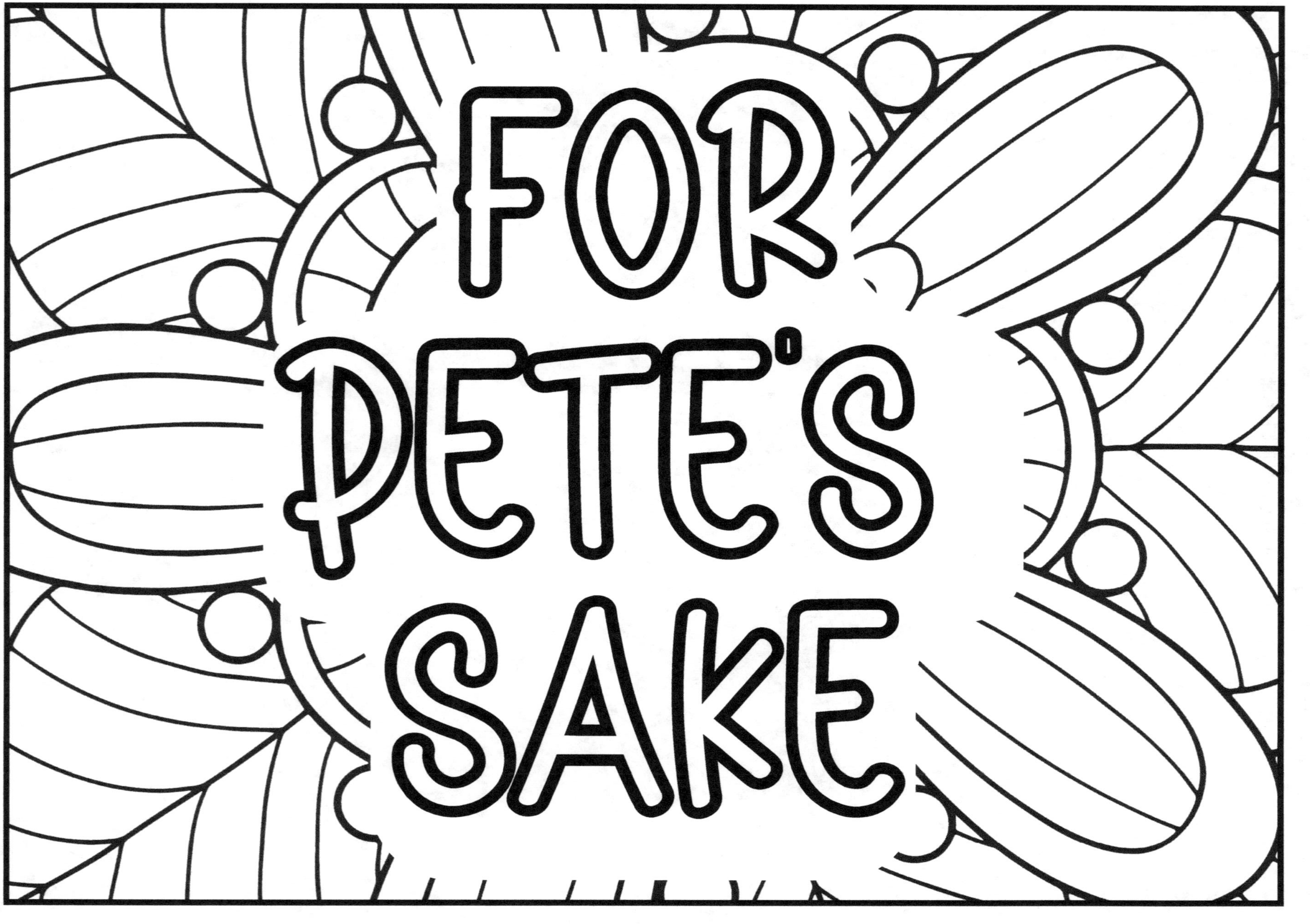
FOR
PETE'S
SAKE

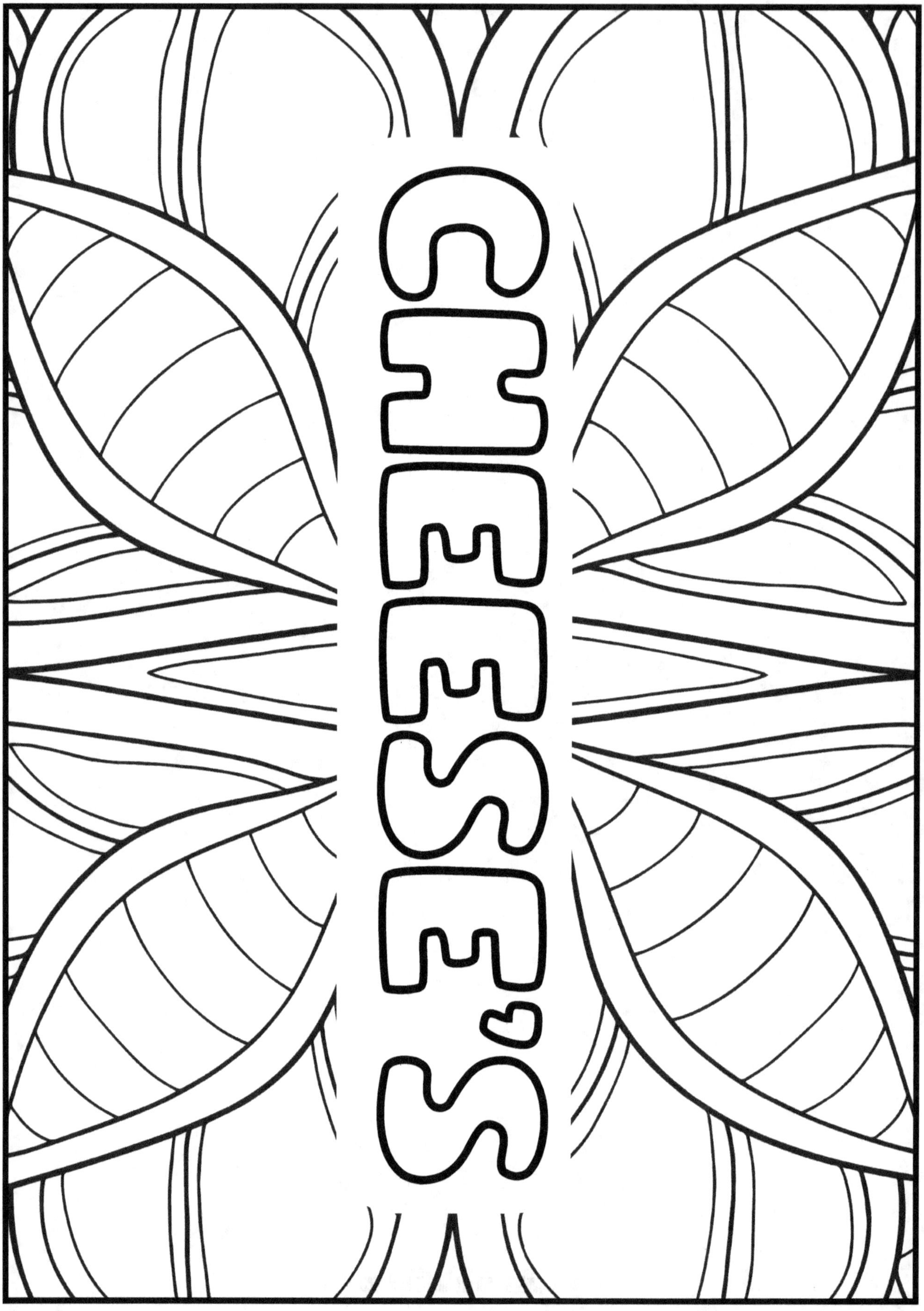
CHEESE'S

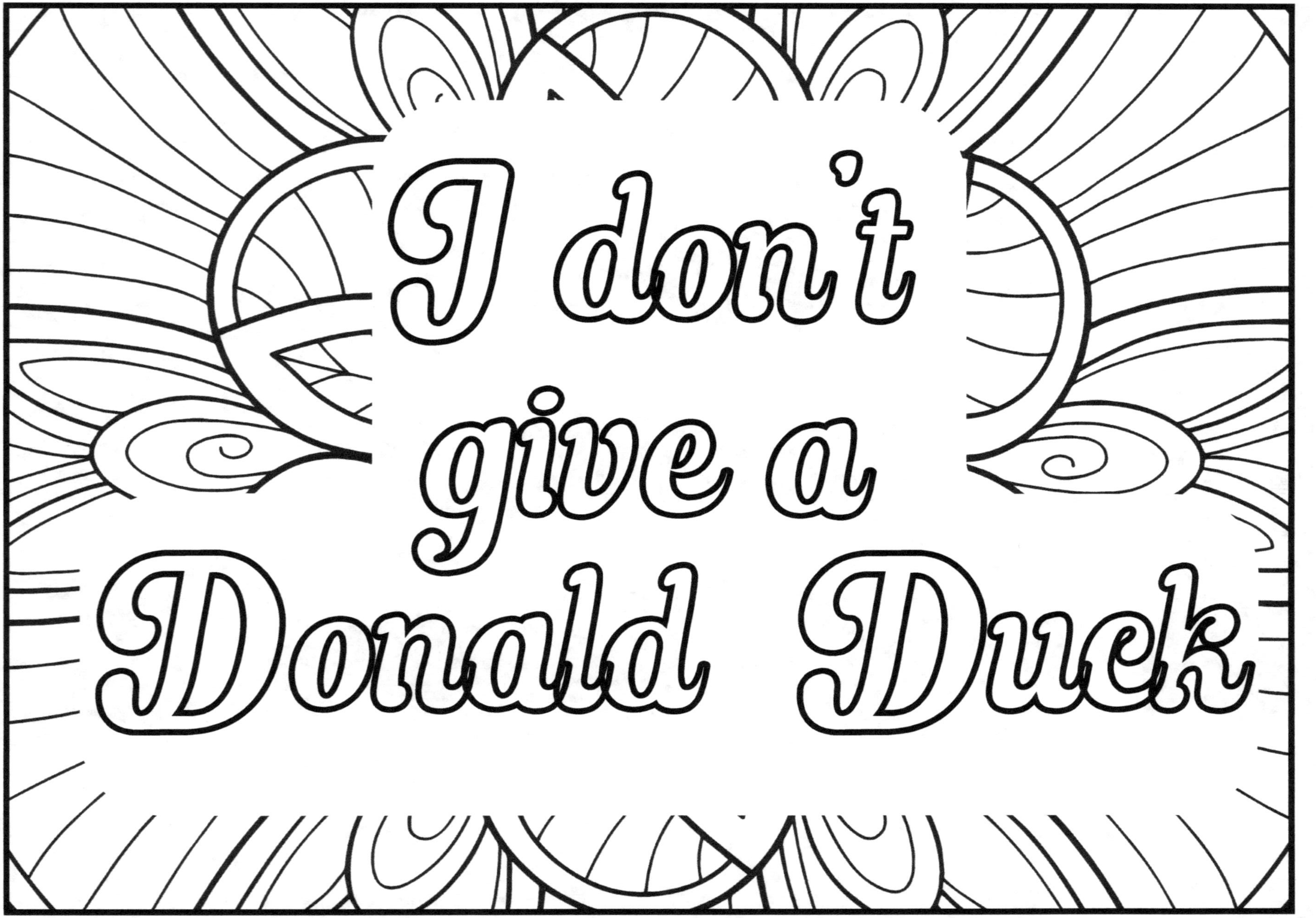
I don't
give a
Donald Duck

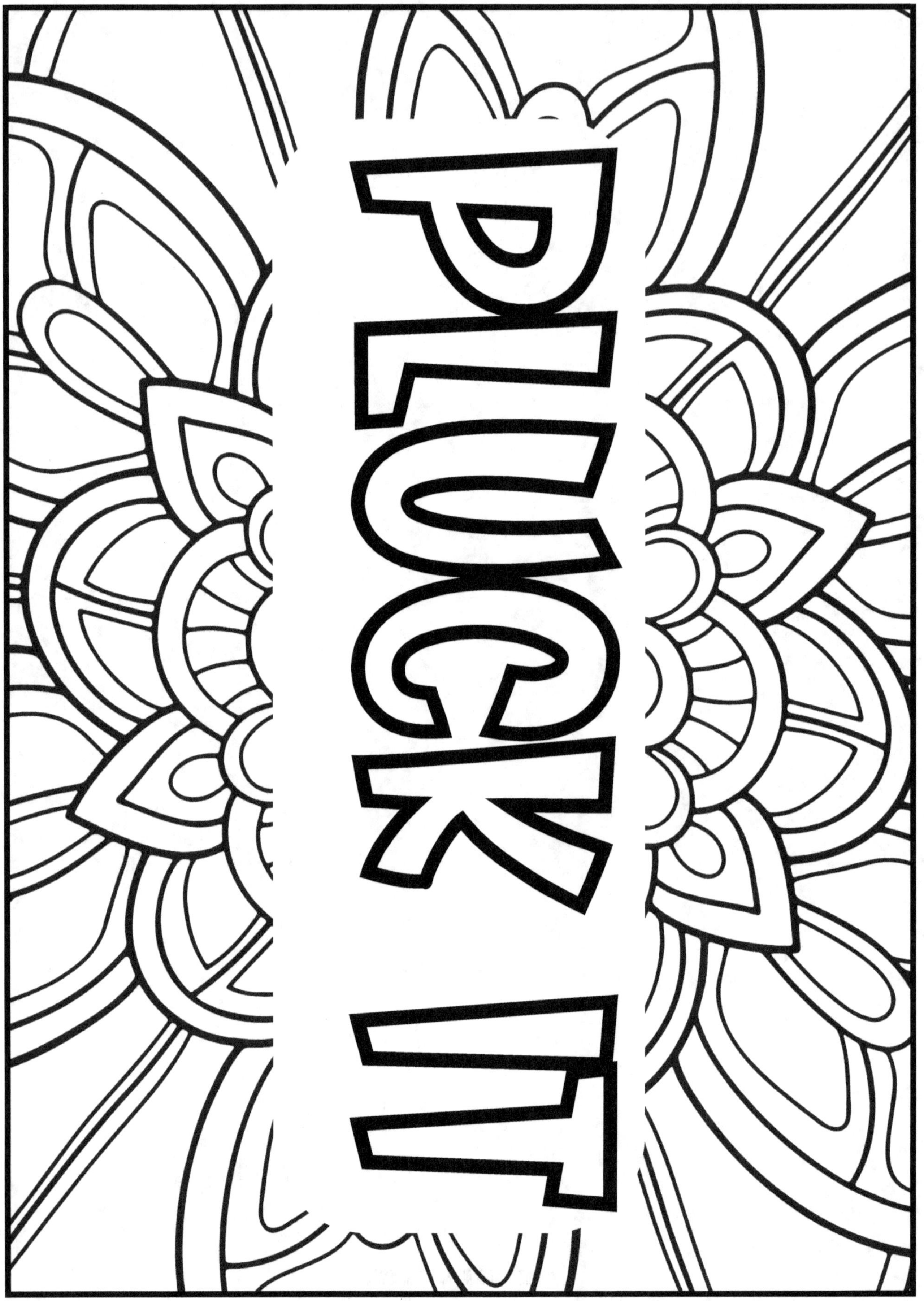
PLUCK IT

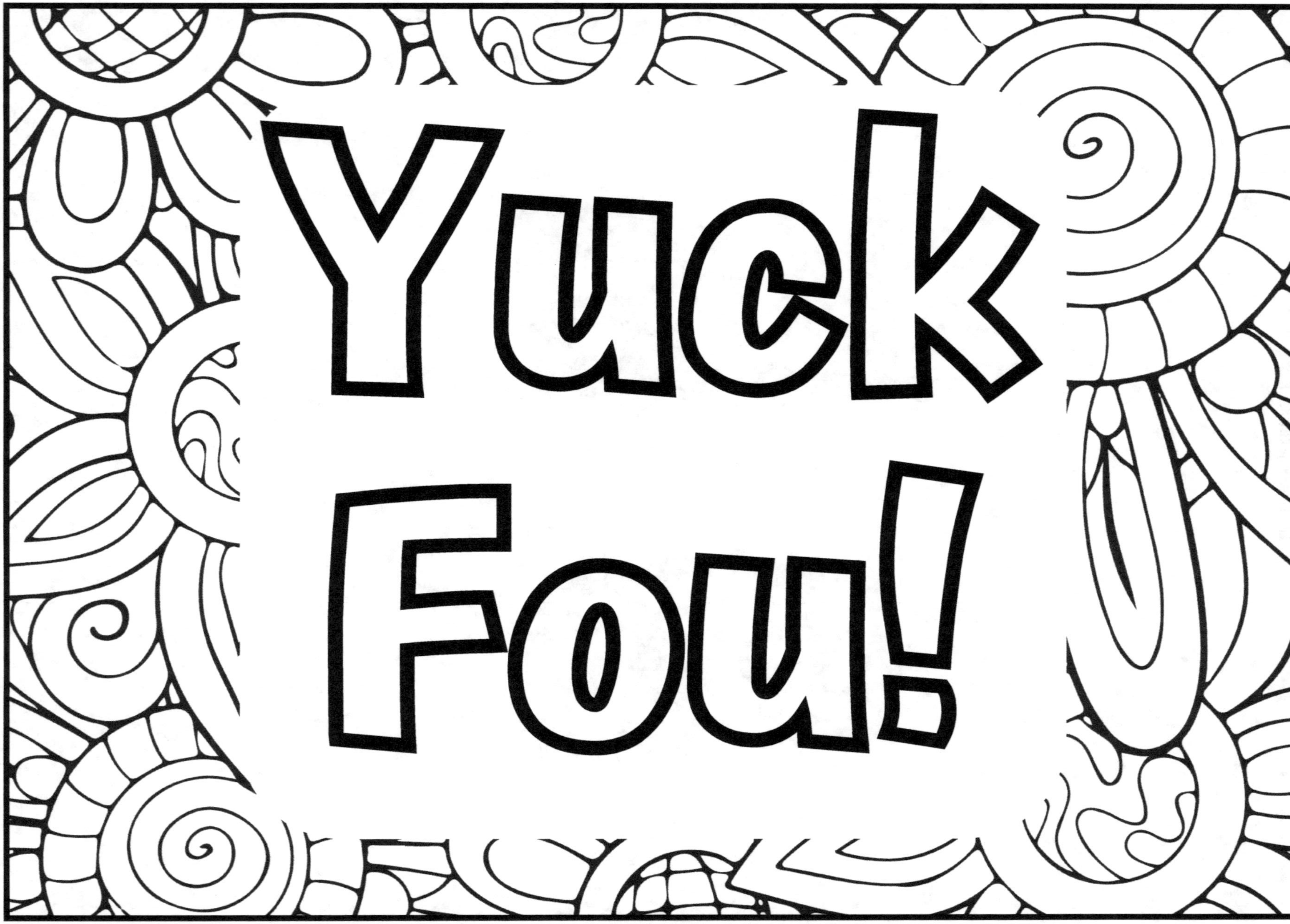
Yuck
Fou!

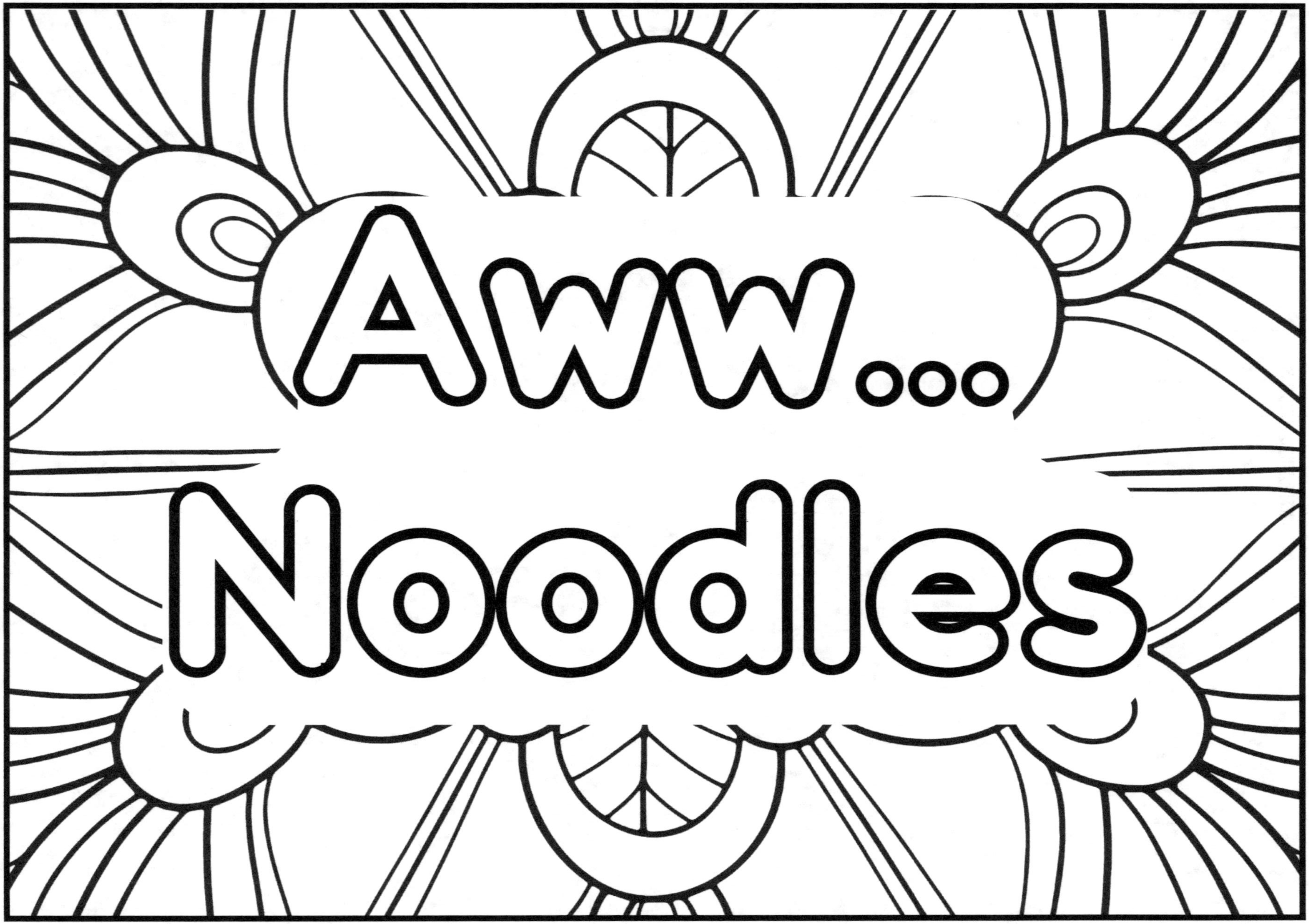
Aww...
Noodles

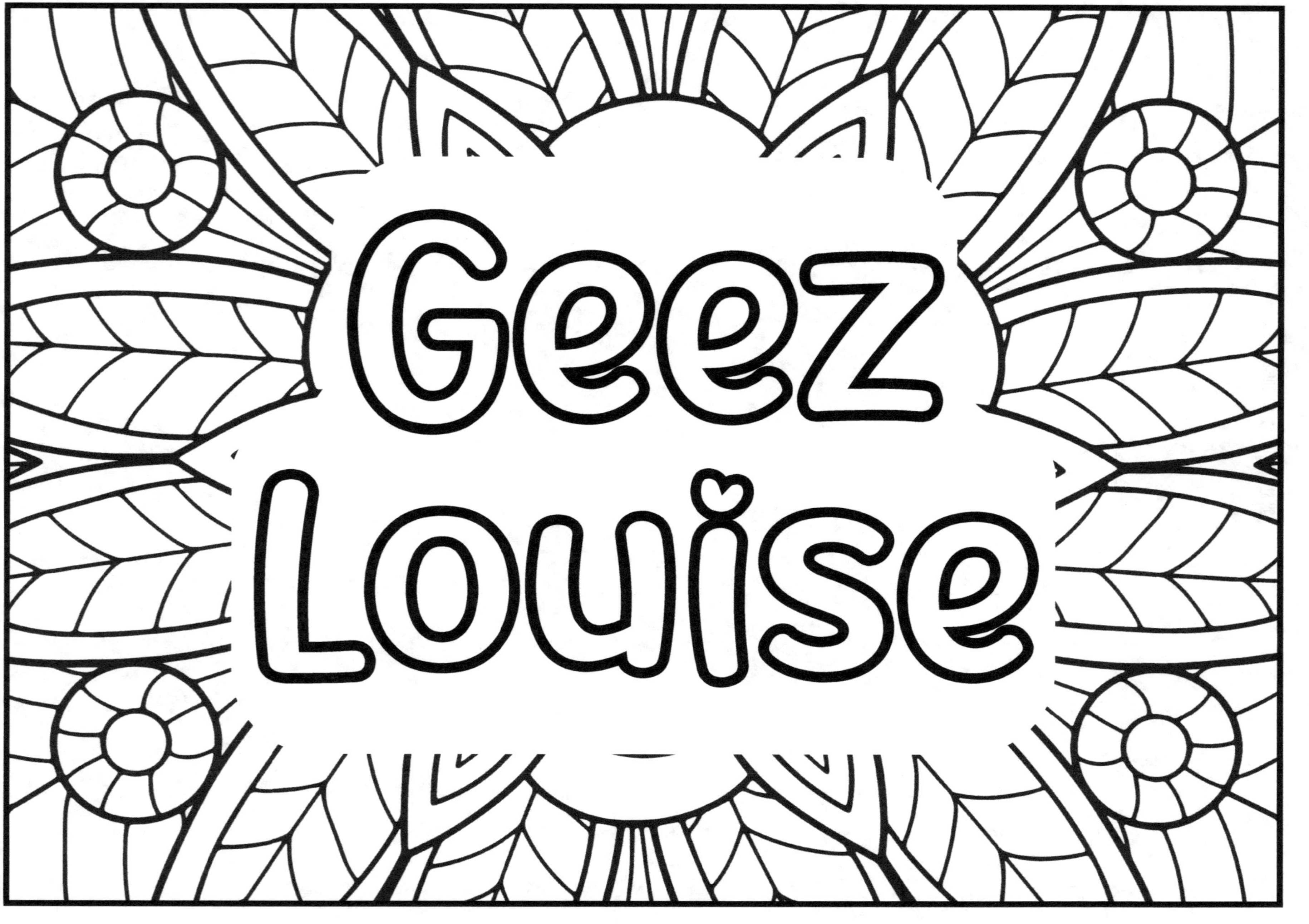
Geez
Louise

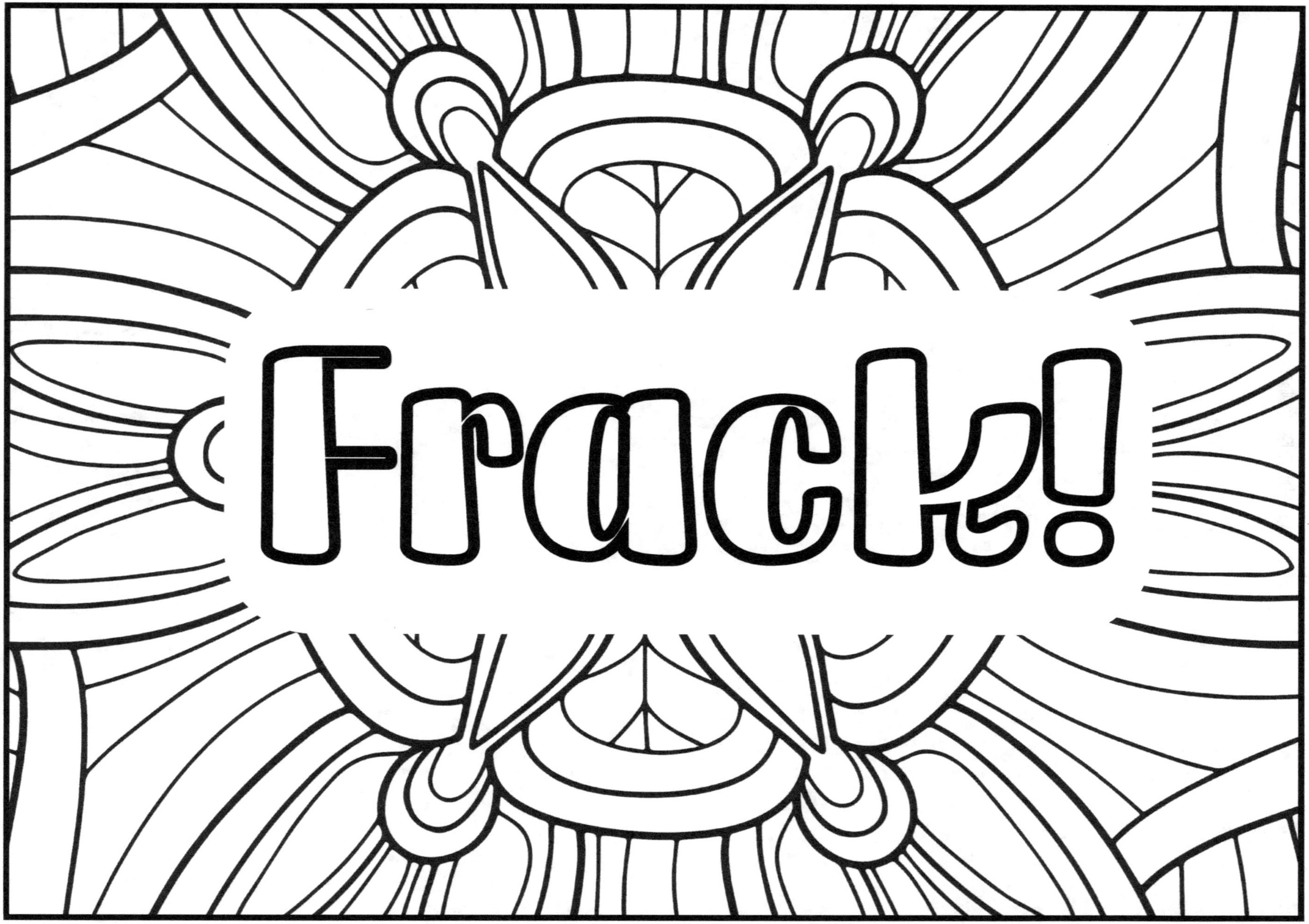
Frack!

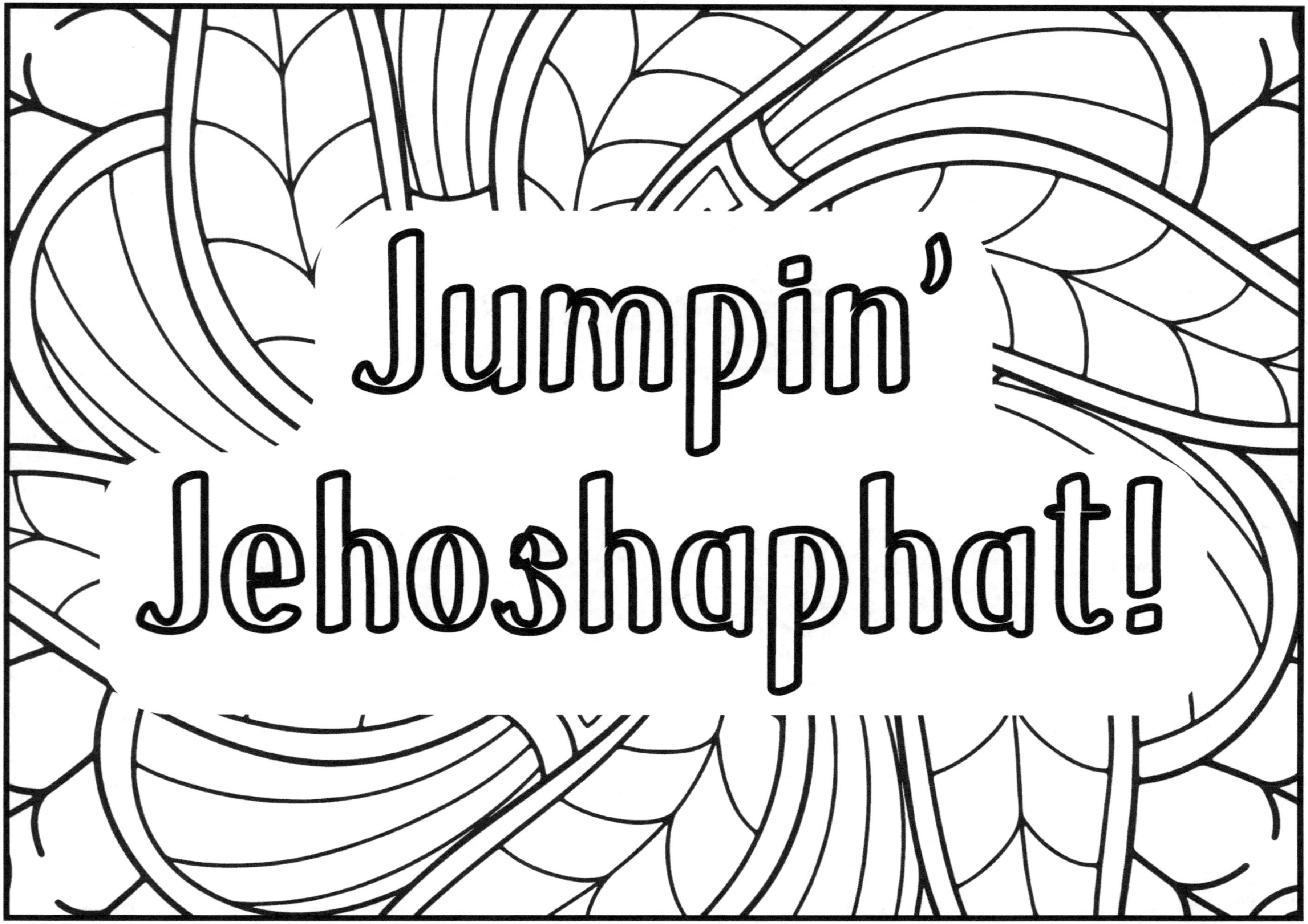
Jumpin'
Jehoshaphat!

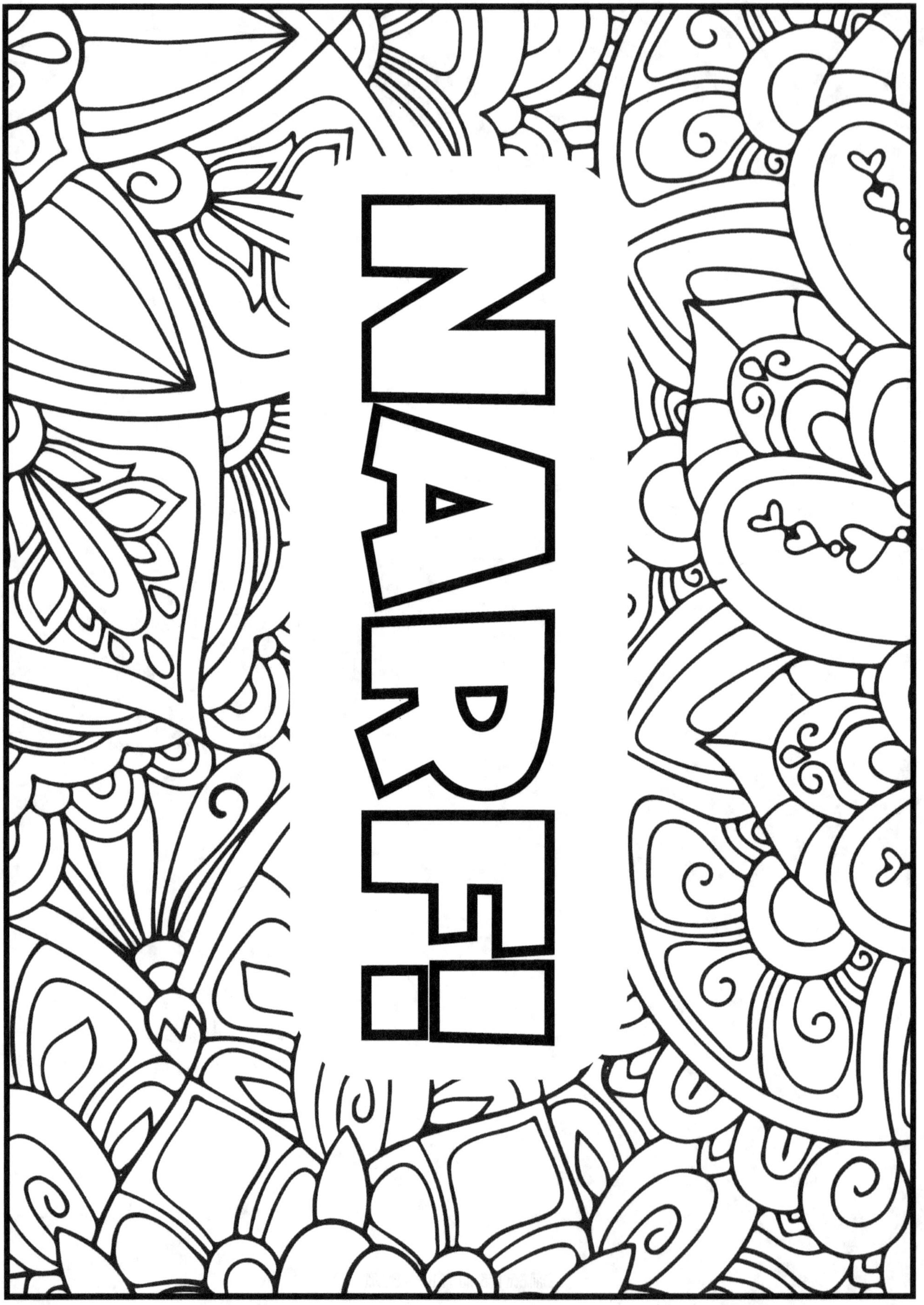
NARF!

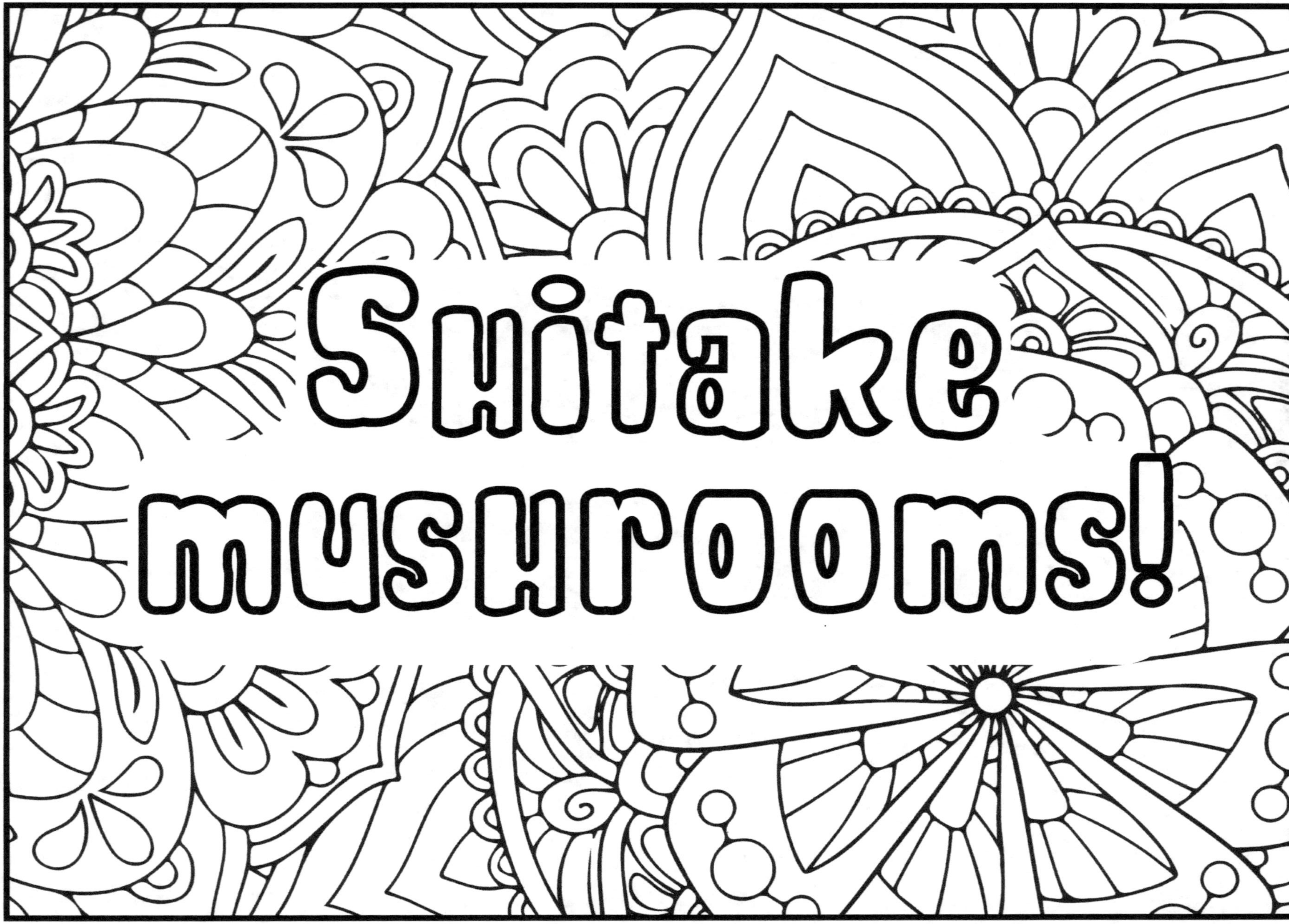
Shitake
mushrooms!

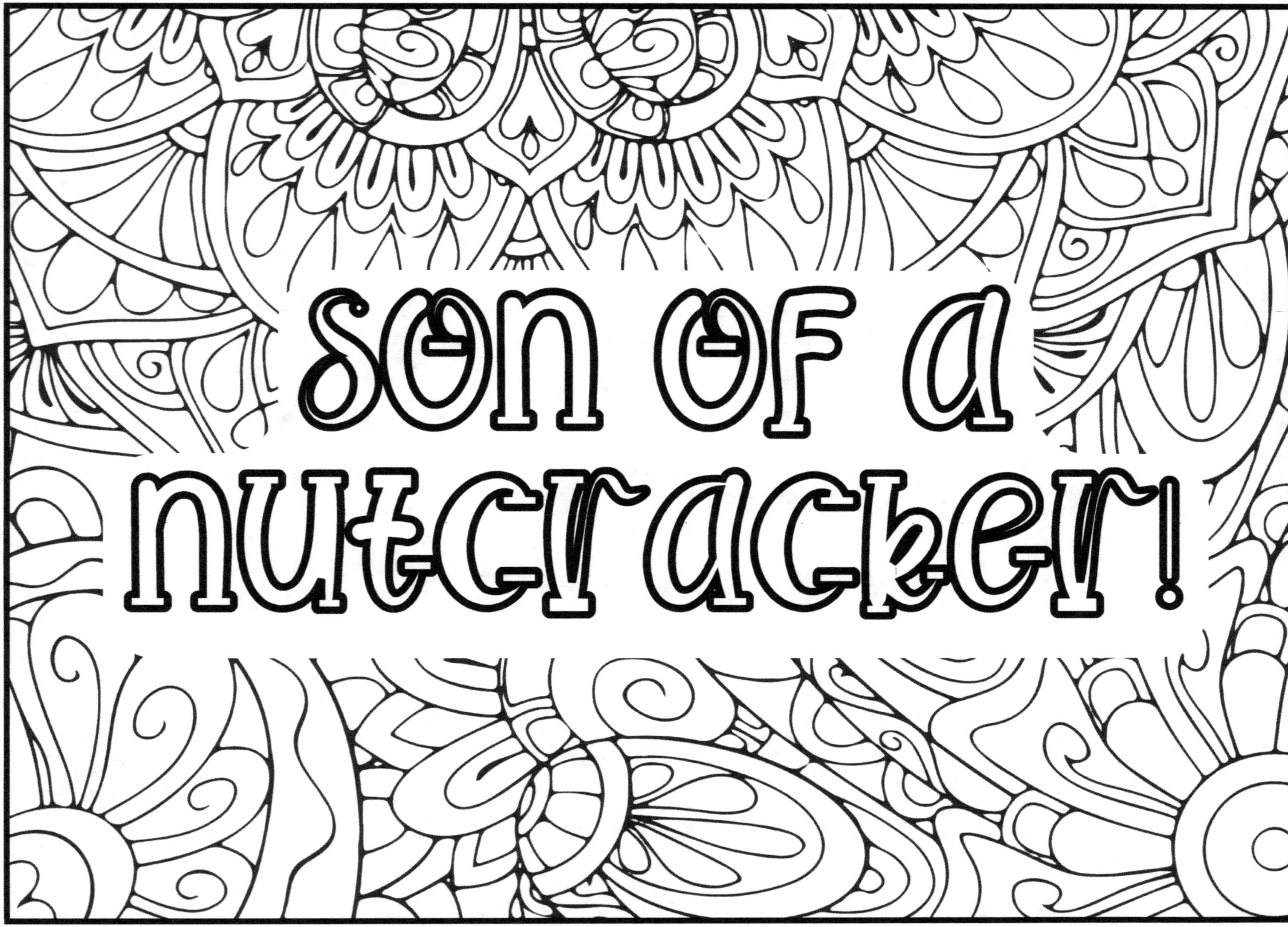
son of a
nutcracker!

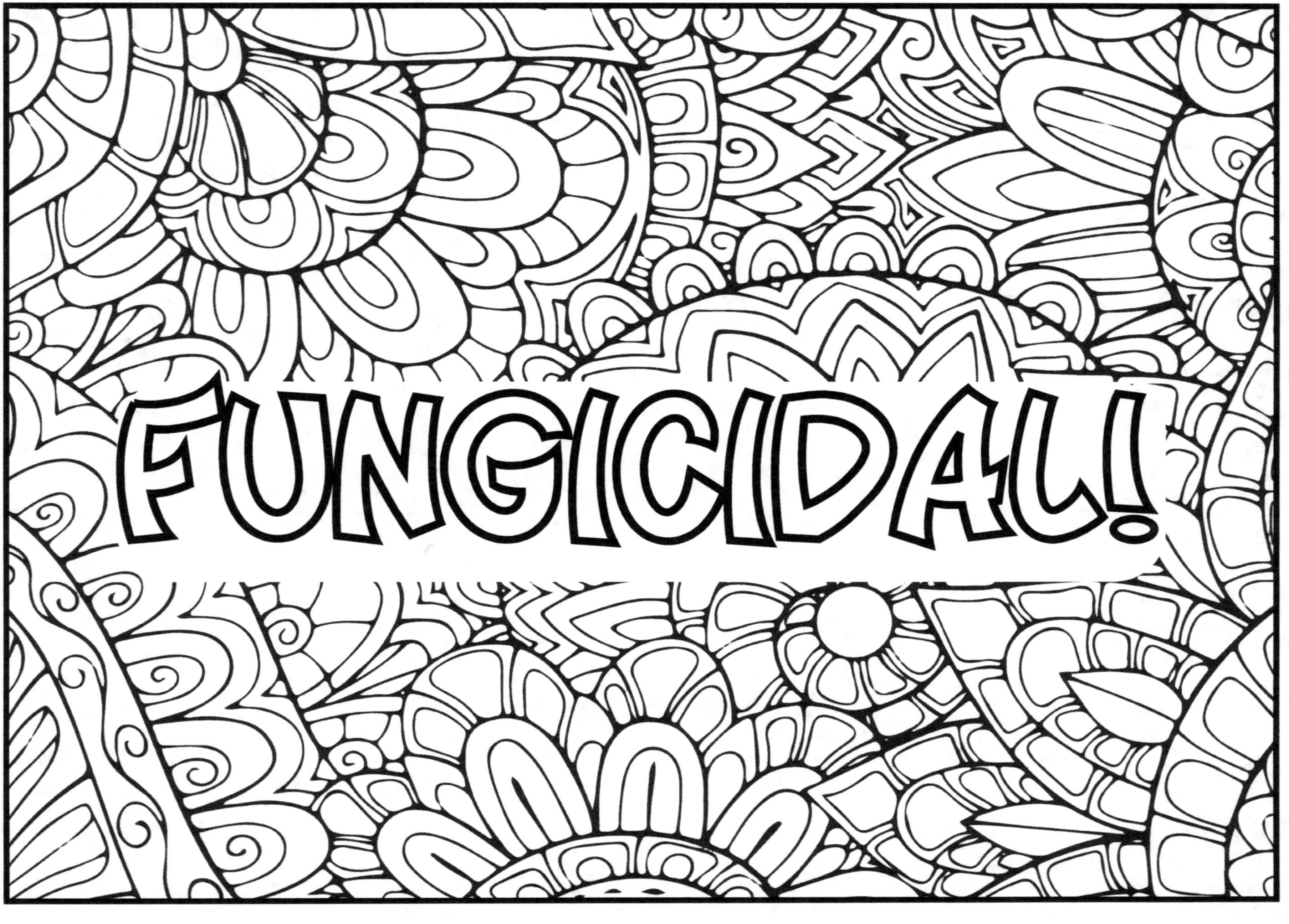
FUNGICIDAL!

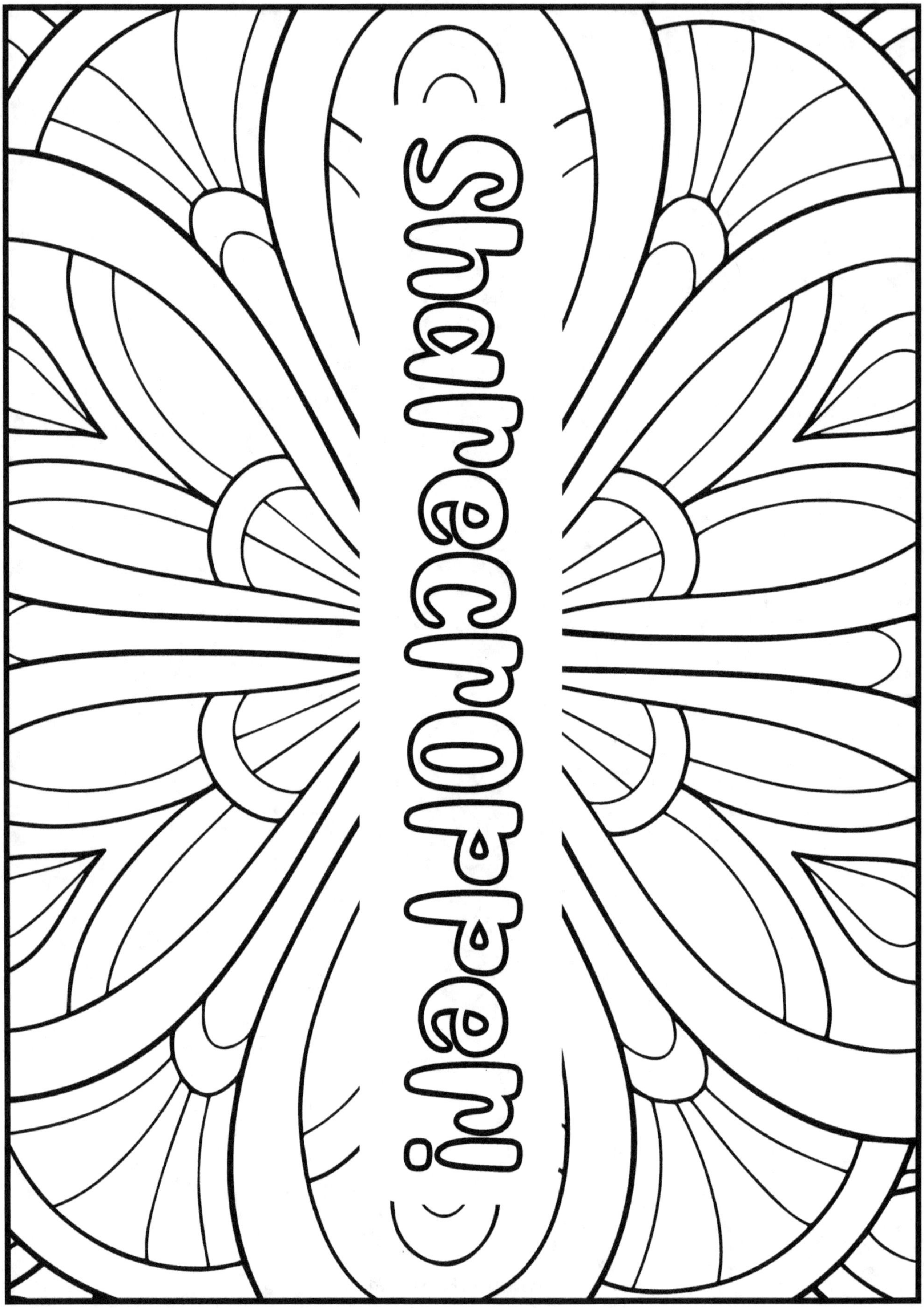
Sharecropper!

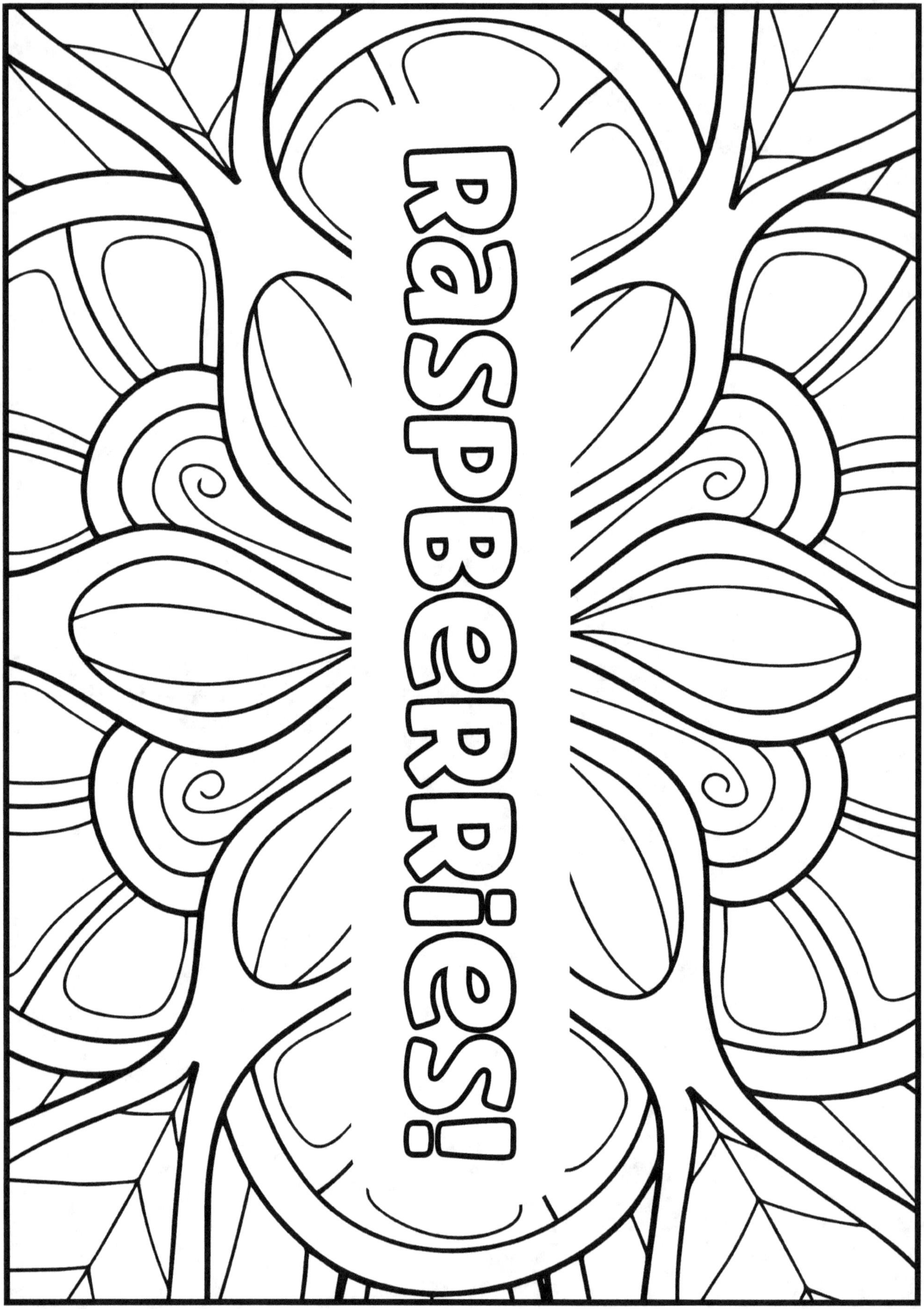
Raspberries!

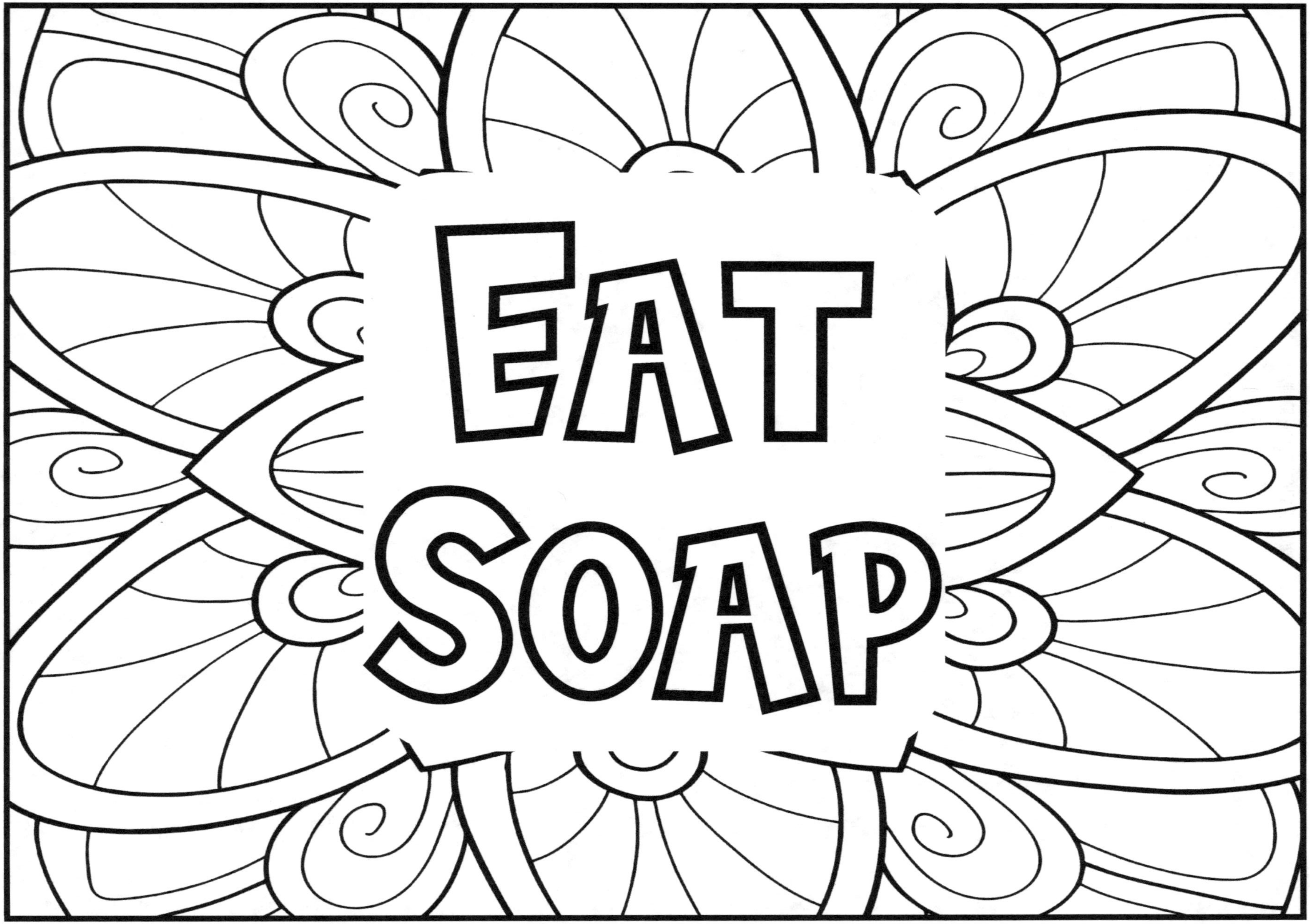
EAT
SOAP

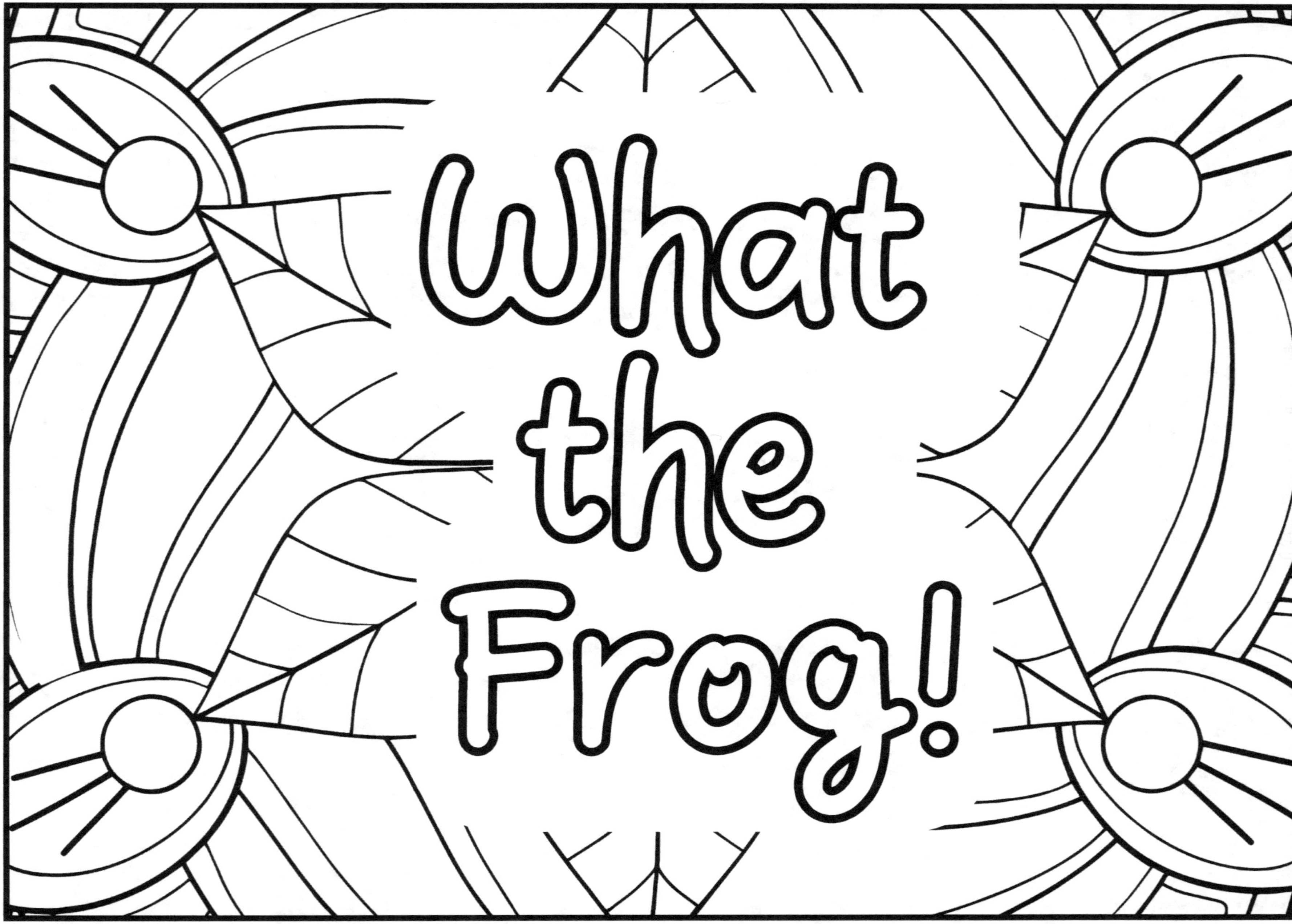
What the Frog!

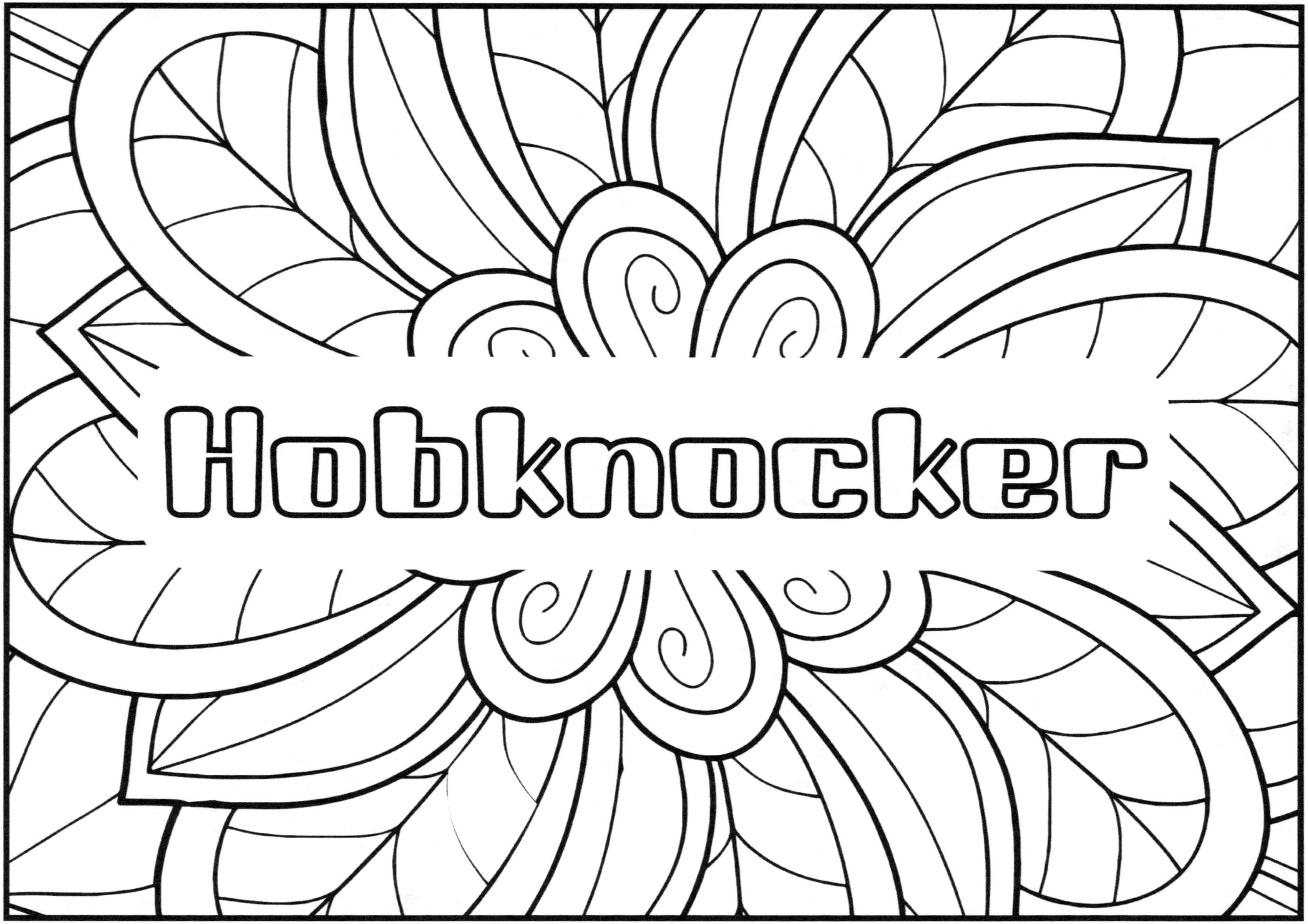
Hobknocker

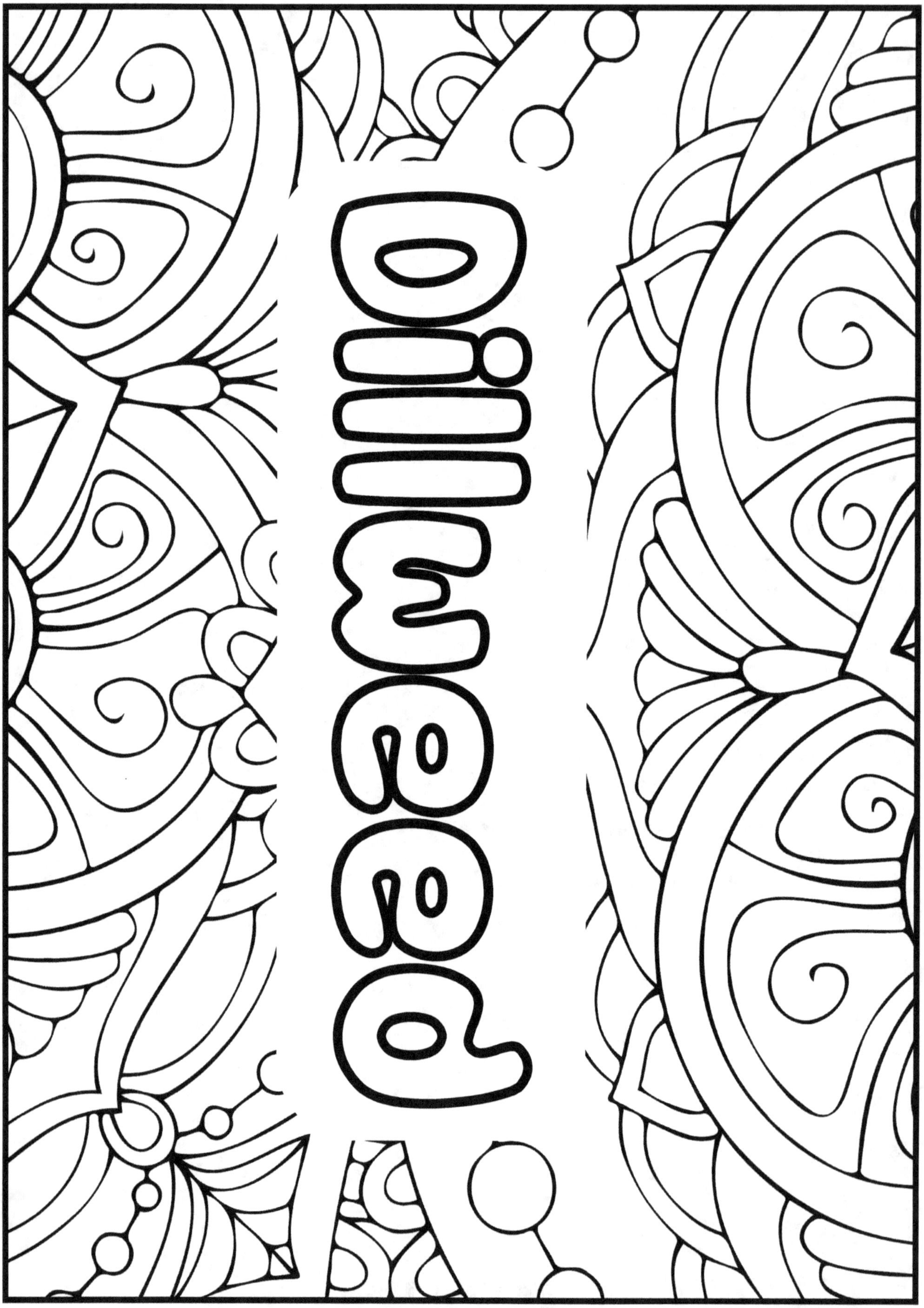
Dillweed

Thank you for all of your support

www.ingramcontent.com/pod-product-compliance
Lightning Source LLC
Chambersburg PA
CBHW062011220526
45467CB00032BA/2253
* 9 7 9 8 3 7 7 9 5 3 1 4 2 *